How Julius Fromm's Condom Empire
Fell to the Nazis

GÖTZ ALY *and* MICHAEL SONTHEIMER

Translated from the German by SHELLEY FRISCH

OTHER PRESS NEW YORK

The translation of this work was supported by a grant from the Goethe-Institut that is funded by the Ministry of Foreign Affairs of the Federal Republic of Germany.

Originally published as Fromms: Wie der jüdische Kondomfabrikant Julius F. unter die deutschen Räuber fiel by Götz Aly and Michael Sontheimer

Production Editor: Yvonne E. Cárdenas
Book design: Simon M. Sullivan
This book was set in 10.25pt Scala by Alpha Design & Composition of Pittsfield, NH.

10 9 8 7 6 5 4 3 2 1

LIBRARY OF CONGRESS CATALOGING-IN-PUBLICATION DATA

Aly, Götz, 1947–
  Fromms : how Julius Fromm's condom empire fell to the Nazis / Götz Aly and Michael Sontheimer ; translated from the German by Shelley Frisch.
    p. cm.
  "Originally published as Fromms : Wie der jüdische Kondomfabrikant Julius F. unter die deutschen Räuber fiel by Götz Aly and Michael Sontheimer."
  Includes bibliographical references and index.
  ISBN 978-1-59051-296-8 (hbk.)—ISBN 978-1-59051-377-4 (e-book)
  1. Fromm, Julius, 1883–1945. 2. Fromms Act (Firm)—History. 3. Condom industry—Germany—Berlin—History—20th century. 4. Jewish business-people—Germany—Berlin—Biography. 5. Aryanization—Germany—Berlin. I. Sontheimer, Michael. II. Frisch, Shelley Laura. III. Title.
  HD9995.C63G33513 2009
  338.7'681761—dc22

                                              2009023468

Contents

GÖTZ ALY: SEX PLUS JEWS

IN THE FALL OF 2004, two colleagues and I were planning to give a reading of unpublished texts. We chose the Sunday Club in the Prenzlauer Berg section of Berlin as our venue. The Sunday Club had been the first gay club to open in the German Democratic Republic, and was now, according to its Web site, a "meeting place for lesbians, gays, and trans-, bi- and heterosexuals."

When it came time to send out announcements, the person in charge of cultural programming asked me whether I really wanted to read the same old "run-of-the-mill hetero claptrap." "Excuse me?" I asked, somewhat taken aback. After all, I had a reputation to uphold. I thought it over for a minute, then remembered that there was a file—hidden away in the vault of the German Democratic Republic Central Bank for decades—that documented the *Entjudung* ("dejudaization," or exclusion of the Jews by the Nazis) at Fromms Act, the condom company in Berlin-Köpenick that had once enjoyed international renown.

I had requested this file several months earlier at the German Federal Archives while investigating another subject. After sifting through it for no more than a few minutes, I realized that it was not pertinent to the topic I was researching, so I returned it to the stacks—quite reluctantly, I might add. The intriguing side issues that emerge by happenstance, the ones archivists gloss over when focusing on what they deem to be the major themes in cataloguing their holdings, are what make historiography such a captivating pursuit. Of course, these side issues, with their many enticing twists and turns, make it nearly impossible for researchers to stay on track. There is no escaping this dilemma. Historians who immerse themselves in source material are bound to veer from their self-prescribed paths.

The staff at the Sunday Club was intrigued by the combination of National Socialism, condoms, sex, and Judaism, and we agreed on the topic. But apart from my chance discovery, I was unable to obtain any other expropriation or restitution files pertaining to Julius Fromm, the founder of the company; the archives in Potsdam and Berlin would not release them. Evidently there was still pending litigation. But I did find the address of Edgar Fromm in London, an heir of the late condom manufacturer. I wrote to him requesting permission to examine the files. As it turned out, the addressee had been dead for the past five years.

This is how I launched my research on a topic that until recently I had deemed immaterial and far too specialized. My thanks go to my coreaders at the event, Martin Z. Schröder and Gustav Seibt, and especially to Pedro at the Sunday Club. It was his provocative intervention that sent me on a rewarding byway, a byway that would shed new light on the events of the twentieth century.

It led me to one of the many Jewish businesses that went under during the National Socialist era and are almost universally ignored by historians. It is not hard to figure out why: because these companies were unceremoniously destroyed, they cannot sponsor business historians, who prefer to follow the money. Over the past twenty years, scholarly interest guided by this monetary inequity has produced a peculiar asymmetry, with the perpetrators and profiteers dominating historical inquiry. The companies' legal successors have supported research because their professed interest in "coming to terms with" an unappealing past fosters their image and thus the marketing of their brands; among the many cases in point are Volkswagen, Krupp, Allianz, Daimler-Benz, Deutsche Bank, Degussa, Dresdner Bank, Flick, and Bertelsmann. Because business history functions in this manner, a giant of the twentieth century like Julius Fromm, the creator of the world's first brand-name condom, seemed destined for oblivion.

Julius Fromm has not even found a place in the lexicon of emigration from German-speaking countries. This book is dedicated to his life's work, his talent, his creative spirit, and his zest for modernity.

Julius Fromm, mid-1920s

MICHAEL SONTHEIMER: EDDIE'S MISSION

SOMETIME EARLY IN 1996, I happened to watch a talk show that featured a captivating elderly gentleman named Edgar Fromm, who was describing how his father, Julius, had made condoms the most popular form of contraception in Germany in the 1920s.

When I was growing up in West Berlin in the 1960s, I learned most of what I knew about the facts of life on the streets. I knew what a "Fromms" was, of course—that was what you called condoms back then. The plural form was Frommse (or, as some people said, Frommser or Frömmser). Just as Kleenex has come to be synonymous with tissues, the brand name Fromms stood for condoms. What I didn't know then was that the term had originated with a man named Julius Fromm, a German Jew who had to flee Berlin in 1938 and emigrate to England.

One of the perks of professional journalism is getting paid to follow leads of your own choosing. I pitched the topic of the history of the Berlin condom manufacturer for a special issue of *Der Spiegel* magazine we were putting together on the theme of love. The next thing I knew, I was sitting in the living room of a small house in London, in upscale Hampstead Garden Suburb in North West London, where many Jews who had fled Germany and Austria in the 1930s had settled. It was here that Edgar Fromm was living with his partner, Lisa Abramson. She had emigrated to London from Danzig in 1937. Both were widowed, and were happily devoted to each other.

Over a good whiskey, Edgar Fromm recounted what he knew about his father and the Fromms Act company. He spoke in an elegant German that sounded somewhat old-fashioned. He regarded my article about his father, Julius, to whom he owed so much, as a belated means of setting the record straight. He told me, in English, what he hoped to achieve: "To put him back on the map." More documents turned up in archives than could be accommodated in a magazine piece, and so a plan to write a book about the history of Fromms Act began to evolve.

It is quite unusual for journalists to strike up a friendship with their sources, but I continued to visit Eddie and Lisa in London at least once a year, and we got together whenever they came to Berlin. Here, in Edgar's hometown, we sought and found the grave of his grandparents and of a cousin at the Jewish cemetery in Weissensee.

When Edgar Fromm died unexpectedly in Baden-Baden in the summer of 1999, I had a guilty conscience. Now he would no longer be able to experience public recognition of his father's achievements, and my motivation to work on the book was gone. The files gathered dust in a corner.

When I visited Lisa Abramson in London six years later, in February 2005, she told me that she had received a letter addressed to Eddie from a historian in Berlin requesting information about Fromms Act. The sender was Götz Aly, with whom I had worked in the early 1980s at the *Tageszeitung* newspaper. We spoke on the phone and decided to write the book together.

Neither Fromm's personal papers nor his company's archives survived the upheavals of emigration, bombing attacks, and the postwar period of psychological and physical rebuilding with its propensity for tossing things away. Among the few documents to surface were two wills Julius Fromm had drawn up, two brief personal letters, two applications to the Potsdam chief administrative officer in his—initially unsuccessful—quest for German citizenship, and, finally, a businesslike letter to the police commissioner in Berlin that kept his denaturalization as an *Ostjude* (Eastern European Jew) at bay in 1934. We managed, in addition, to obtain certificates, marketing materials, and photographs that helped us construct a picture of Julius Fromm, and we spoke to the few remaining people who could give us information about him. We compiled these fragments to reconstruct his profile— to put him back on the map.

Frankfurt and Berlin, October 2006

FROMMS

JULIUS FROMM, SEX, AND FAMILY PLANNING

THERE IS ONLY ONE REMAINING MEMBER of the Fromm family who knew Julius Fromm well—and she did not like him. This person is Ruth Fromm, born in Berlin in 1919, a daughter of Julius's older brother Salomon. Diminutive and delicate at the age of eighty-seven, and ebullient despite her arthritis, she lives in Manhattan and speaks a wonderfully old-fashioned Berlin-tinged German. Of course she often switches back to English, and then, out of nowhere, punctuates descriptions of her diet and the dangers of bird flu with a high-pitched giggle. Although she never had children, she is the glue that binds the Fromm family—a family "scattered all over the planet."

Ruth knows a great many stories about the living and the deceased relatives in Johannesburg, Berlin, Paris, Munich, and London. She enjoys chatting about Aunt Helene, a merry widow, and the most high-spirited of Julius Fromm's seven siblings. Before the war, Helene ran an optician's shop in Berlin. Indulging in a bit of word play with the family name Fromm, which in

German means "pious," and throwing in a reference to the title of a famous German poem by Wilhelm Busch, Ruth declares that this aunt was anything but a "pious Helene" (*fromme Helene*): "She knew how to deal with men."

There is one member of the family Ruth does not want to speak about: Uncle Julius. She does not have a single picture of him in her photo collection. It feels as though you have to grill her to unearth any information about him. She eventually volunteers that he was a cold individual, in marked contrast to her many other kindhearted uncles and aunts. He was fixated on his business, on money, on the company. "There is nothing more to be said about him." We will come back to the reasons why Ruth still bears a grudge, but there is certainly a great deal more to be said about Julius Fromm.

———

A rosier view, albeit along similar lines, was offered in a March 1933 public tribute to Julius Fromm on the occasion of his fiftieth birthday, a scant few weeks after the Nazis came to power in Germany. This tribute appeared in the drugstore trade journal *Der Drogenhändler*: "It has taken him exceedingly intense, single-minded devotion to his work to get to where he is today. We all pay tribute to his impressive and brilliant lifetime achievements. The untimely death of his father drove him to seek his own way at an early age, and to give his life a meaning and a direction of his own design." He was the kind of businessman, the tribute went on to say, who understood the importance of "keeping the company permanently under his control," and the firm's "colossal modern buildings" conveyed a sense of "the international status that German workplaces enjoy." "Ample publicity, exceptional customer service, and, above all, consistent high quality have earned the 'Fromms Act' brand the complete trust and satisfaction of customers."[1]

A more permissive attitude toward sexuality had begun to develop during World War I, and grew more pronounced during the turbulent early years of the Weimar Republic. Symptomatic of a newfound tolerance for physical intimacy was the dance mania that swept through every social class in Germany. Even the 1919 memorial service for the murdered communist Karl Liebknecht was followed by a "tea dance." As part of a new trend in science, institutes outside the walls of academe founded the modern field of sexology. The historian Walter Laqueur's book on this era describes a "new sex wave" that extended "to nude shows and hard-core pornography." Berlin began to copy Paris; small French-style nightclubs shot up out of nowhere, and erotic pulp fiction was all the rage, with topics including nights in a harem, women and whips, courtesans' erotic apprenticeships, luscious ladies, boys' love letters, gynecologists' diaries, lesbian women ("feminine eroticism swinging the other way"), and vicissitudes in the garden of love.

Julius Fromm, late 1920s

The Reich Business Machine Dealers' Association held a beauty contest for stenographers, and "Berlin's latest attraction" debuted in the early 1930s: a sexology bookshop on Wittenbergplatz. A protest pamphlet was quick to report: "The word 'sexual,' in huge blue-and-silver Roman-style letters, stares passersby in the face. All day long, people crowd around the display windows." This "prominent feature of the shop" quickly resulted in "repeated visits by the police." In December 1932, a court sentenced the owner to eight months for "distributing lewd literature."[2]

It was at this time that Julius Fromm was advertising his new "select brand." While this innovative contraceptive device, sheerer and less intrusive than earlier products of its kind, had been developed for personal use, it had far-reaching consequences for the fabric of society as a whole. The condoms helped to eliminate the traditional unity of sexuality and reproduction, and facilitated promiscuity, sexual experimentation, and eroticism liberated from the confines of everyday family life.

Consequently, the chairman of the Fulda Bishops' Conference, Adolf Cardinal Bertram, launched an attack on this contraceptive device in 1921, calling it "an incentive to fornicate." Condom advertising, he inveighed, would "obfuscate or obliterate the moral precepts of our nation," and result in "a plummeting birthrate" and "the loss of the noblest strength of our nation." Magnus Hirschfeld, one of the founders of modern sexology, saw the matter quite differently, and expressed his great admiration for Fromms Act: "This is a leading company in Berlin; day after day, no fewer than 144,000 prophylactic devices are produced, and even then the company can barely keep up with the demand for this product."

Magnus Hirschfeld emphasized the menace posed by venereal diseases—syphilis in particular—and expounded on all the misery, "the diseases and germs [that had been] 'nipped in the

4

bud' by these products." Few companies had had "such a profound impact on human sexuality and social interaction" as Fromms Act, the legendary factory with the proud (if somewhat ambiguous) name. After taking a tour of Fromm's factory in 1926, Hirschfeld concluded: "To the best of my knowledge and principles, and in the light of my practical experience and theoretical deliberations, the prophylactics distributed under the Fromms Act label optimally fulfill all prerequisites for a suitable protective and preventive prophylactic device."

————

A modest dip in the birthrate in Germany was recorded beginning in 1875. This decline accelerated rapidly after the turn of the century, and was generally attributed to the "rationalization of sexual life," a phrase coined by the economist Julius Wolf in a 1912

Advertisement in a pharmaceutical trade journal, 1930

study bearing that title. Wolf concluded that "increased aware-
ness of birth control methods, improved technological 'advance-
ment,' and greater accessibility to birth control have provided
considerable momentum for the plummeting birth rate."

An increasing number of Germans in urban areas began moving to a "two-child system" (and after World War I even to a "one-
child system")—to the dismay not only of Catholic dignitaries, but
also of many demographers and politicians. This shift was soon
evident in rural areas as well. The German Jews were at the fore-
front of the new demographic pattern. The 1927 edition of the
Jewish Lexicon reported: "Despite a 29 percent increase in mar-
riages over the last 50 years, the number of births in this period
has fallen by over 43 percent." Maintaining the Jewish population of Berlin at the same level would require "a constant influx
of Jewish people from outside the city."[3]

In the early 1930s, an alliance formed between National Socialists bent on "maintaining the nation's strength into the next
generation" and churchgoing fundamentalists committed to
chastity and marital fidelity. Kurt Gerstein became the strident
voice of this motley collaboration. A dedicated member of the
Confessing Church, a Christian resistance movement in Nazi
Germany, who joined the Waffen-SS and attained the rank of
Obersturmführer, he began spying on Nazi operations, and as early
as August 1942 sent the Swedes a highly detailed report about the
death camps of Belzec, Sobibor, Treblinka, and Majdanek, accompanied by a request to relay this information about these
murders to the Allies. Just a few years prior, though, in 1936,
Gerstein had issued an anti-Semitic statement on the need to protect minors, which included the following remark about condom
advertisements: "One need look no further than the brand name
'Primeros' (meaning 'first love') to grasp the skulduggery of this
disgraceful business cooked up by the Jews. . . . Furthermore,

there should be a ban on the sale of these devices in vending machines, which are doing a brisk business. These machines, which have sealed the fate of many a curious young person, were also introduced in Germany by a Jewish company." Incidentally, Primeros condoms were manufactured by a Saxon-Bohemian company named Emil Schuran.

In 1928, after protracted opposition, Julius Fromm had finally succeeded in his ongoing efforts to install the first condom vending machines. He promoted his product with the slogan: "Men, Protect Your Health." The Social Democratic minister of justice, Gustav Radbruch, had prohibited wording that included any reference to sexual pleasure or pregnancy prevention. Privy Councillor Martin Fassbender, a representative of the Center Party in the Prussian parliament, warned that vending machines of this sort would inundate "young people [with] erotic stimuli."

In 1936 Gerstein submitted a written statement in a futile attempt to avoid expulsion from the Nazi Party and consequent dismissal from civil service. This statement stressed his outstanding service on the moral front: "Furthermore, I would like to point out that I have spent years fighting against Jewish-Bolshevist attacks on the power of the German people. . . . The minister of the interior is in possession of files relating to my years of attacks on Fromms Act and Primeros, those companies owned by the disgraceful Jewish-Galician swine, which distributed millions of free samples to very young adolescents."

During the years of the Weimar Republic, Gerstein and his comrades-in-arms had formed a small grassroots organization with a long name, the Reichsschundkampfstelle der evangelischen Jungmännerbünde Deutschlands (Reich Anti-Smut Campaign Bureau of Protestant Young Men's Associations of Germany). This organization published a leaflet called "Der Schundkampf" ("The Fight Against Smut"), aimed at "banning advertisements for risqué books, sex education pamphlets, condom products, and other health-related articles" and items of that nature, and "stricter monitoring of advertisements for massage parlors and for institutes teaching foreign languages." A similar campaign was conducted by the Volkswartbund (People's Surveillance League), which described itself as "a Catholic association to fight public displays of lewdness."

In 1925 the Protestant Reichsschundkampfstelle came out with a set of "Ten Commandments for Combating Licentiousness." The third "commandment" stipulated: "Do not support any Jewish or yellow-press publications." On May 10, 1933, this group sprang into action at the Berlin book burnings by setting aflame books it considered lewd: "While students from the Berlin School for Physical Education purged the library of the Magnus Hirschfeld Institute, the Protestant *Schundkämpfer* purged about ten municipal and seventy private libraries in a single day. There was a huge yield. It took two trucks to transport some 1,212 books (which included the worst kind of filth) to Opernplatz for the solemn conflagration. The fire set by the students is just the beginning of this purge. We will systematically continue this clean-up effort." Buoyed by their own success in this enterprise, and by the new political opportunities that lay ahead, the devoted activists reported that "when Dr. Goebbels gave the signal to attack, Protestant *Schundkämpfer* were mobilized in more than forty German cities to cleanse public and private libraries."[4]

In 1914, when Julius Fromm began manufacturing condoms in Wilhelmine Germany, men were quite bashful about asking for prophylactics at the barber shop or the drugstore. Their source was generally shrouded in mystery, and the quality dubious. But demand grew quickly. As the number of patients suffering from incurable syphilis continued to rise, the doctors sounded the alarm and sought to popularize condoms with epidemiological arguments. In 1913, when the Reichstag debated a law to restrict "commerce pertaining to birth control methods," the German Association for Obstetrics and Gynecology was horrified. "In our view," wrote five prominent gynecologists in Berlin, "neither a prohibition nor even a mere limitation of the distribution of condoms can be considered, because they promote good health above and beyond their contraceptive purpose." They went on to argue that a substantial increase in venereal disease would inevitably follow if obtaining this protective device was made more difficult. The experts did agree, though, that "public displays" of contraceptive devices ought to be outlawed.

In 1912 the Royal Prussian Ministry of the Interior investigated the causes of the decline in the birthrate and determined that "town and country" were "virtually inundated with advertising, price lists, and such, promoting items described as 'rubber goods,' 'prophylactics,' 'sanitary products,' etc. . . . time and again emphasizing the 'economic and health drawbacks that came with having too many children' and the need to restrict the number of offspring 'to provide better education for the smaller number of children.'" Engaged couples and newlyweds were being targeted "systematically" to receive brochures conveying the message that modern methods could help them "structure at least the first few years of marriage as pleasantly as possible." This study also revealed that unmarried people were also being sent this kind of advertising, often in the guise of "medical or scientific" information. Moreover, these manufacturers were playing up "the harmlessness of extramarital sex." The ministry officials concluded that once people grew accustomed to using contraceptive devices, they would be "inclined to use them in marriage."[5]

These concerns on the part of the Ministry of the Interior notwithstanding, the condom gained popularity after World War I began, not only in Germany, but throughout Europe and the

German "battlefield brothel" for officers in World War I

United States. Venereal disease epidemics had been causing problems for army leadership even in peacetime, and during this period of modern mass warfare, conventional morality loosened and infection rates shot up. In the German infantry, the number of soldiers infected with syphilis or gonorrhea increased by 25 percent, and in the German occupying forces the rate rose by 100 percent.

The leadership of all armies involved in the war extolled abstinence as a soldierly virtue while acknowledging the reality of the situation. In order to maintain some control over prostitution, they set up soldiers' brothels. Behind the front lines, existing establishments were often taken over and expanded. Near the main battlegrounds, medical service personnel improvised basic field brothels. Many of these dreary facilities made the use of condoms mandatory. A German military doctor in the Warsaw area who was given orders to open a "brothel for the members of formations that came marching through" reported in his memoirs: "The entry fee for officers was three marks; for soldiers, one mark. The price included a condom and a voucher to hand to the girl."

Soldiers' brothel in Galicia

In most cases the brothels for officers were kept strictly separate from those for the rank and file. The upscale bordellos featured signs announcing: "Entry forbidden to dogs and enlisted men!" Ordinary soldiers were required first to display their genitals to Neumann, the legendary medical corporal, and then to register, before joining one of the lines in front of the brothels for enlisted men. The officers were spared any inspection, and consequently the percentage of men infected with venereal disease was markedly higher in this group. Before long there was a shortage of condoms. It is no coincidence that 1916 was the year that Fromms Act began its ascent as a modern industrial enterprise.

After the war, many patients told Max Marcuse, a sexologist in Berlin, that they had become more prudent while in the army. Men from the country in particular used condoms for the first time in their lives when they became soldiers. The idea was to prevent venereal disease, and in the process they learned about family planning. Public health officials at the Ministry of the

Interior began predicting as early as 1916: "After the war, return-
ing soldiers and other individuals, faced with uncertainty about
the economic situation, will be even more inclined to use contraceptive devices, thereby preventing a rise in the number of children." In the *Concise Dictionary of Sexology* Marcuse edited in
1923, the "widely available" condom was listed as "the safest
contraceptive device, relatively speaking," and the dictionary
claimed it ought to be considered "virtually harmless for men
and women."[6]

––––

The Reichstag had been considering passage of a law to combat
venereal disease since 1916. After much debate, the law, which
would permit the use of advertising for condoms, was slated to
go into effect on October 1, 1923. At the eleventh hour, however,
conservative forces were able to postpone its promulgation in the
Reichsgesetzblatt ("Reich Law Gazette") until February 18, 1927,
and to add restrictions to paragraph 11—the crux of the law—to
prohibit any public advertising of condoms. A violation of this rule
could result in up to six months' imprisonment. The only exception was advertising in professional journals intended for readers "officially permitted to do business involving these devices or
objects." On the other hand, devices "that serve to prevent venereal diseases" could be "displayed and promoted." The condom
fell into both categories—it was a contraceptive *and* a protective
device.

   A small advertisement in a popular magazine reading "Married
couples, sanitary items, free price list!" was thus considered legally
suspect even in the Weimar Republic. The German Central Police
Bureau to Stem the Circulation of Lewd Pictures, Literature, and
Advertisements kept an eagle eye on condom advertising to ensure
that it did not become "intrusive" to the public. This special agency,
which had national jurisdiction, was located at Magazinerstrasse

3–5 in Berlin, the very building where the East German State Security Service (Stasi) would later pursue its own kind of "clean living" campaign, this time of a political nature, for it was here that the Stasi compiled the notorious "Brown Book" listing "War and Nazi Criminals in West Germany."

In view of the legal situation, condom advertising had to focus solely on protection against venereal disease. The contraceptive function was not mentioned, since the law considered language on that subject a "public incitement to indecency," and made it punishable with a prison sentence. Consequently, the advertisement carried only this vague wording: "Fromms Act—Against Infection. Available at All Specialty Stores."[7] Julius Fromm waited until 1932 to promote the "important advantages" of his products, and even then he chose a trade journal for pharmacists:

1. Our select brand, Fromms Act, the top-selling brand in Germany, is not just *labeled* transparent, but truly *is* transparent—a feature that demanding customers value.
2. Our select brand, Fromms Act, has been *dipped evenly* and is guaranteed to have been tested twice to assure reliability.
3. Our select brand, Fromms Act, has *no unpleasant smell*, and is therefore not distracting.
4. Our select brand, Fromms Act, *does not obstruct sensation*; its silky quality does not feel intrusive.

The advertisement also assured readers that the powder used as a lubricant had been "field tested," and contained no "harsh or irritating substances." Shortly before that, the company had found it necessary to take out another large advertisement announcing: "Fromms Act—Advertising Permitted!" Even so, pharmacists were advised: "In the unlikely event that you experience difficulties with the authorities, we ask you to let us know as soon as possible so that we may offer you advice and assistance."[8]

Conditions in the Weimar Republic further destabilized traditional moral strictures. Urbanization, the social mobility that accompanies industrial society, a growing interest in pursuing higher education, and the emancipation of women all fostered a desire not to leave the number of offspring to nature. Then again, prudery and ignorance were still very much in evidence, and for decades to come, Fromms Act packages contained folded inserts that pharmacy customers could push across the counter without needing to state what they wished to purchase. The inserts contained this text: "Please hand me a 3-pack of Fromms' condoms discreetly."

Fromm worked tirelessly to improve what is known in the business as "rubber hollow bodies," and developed new variants that offered no additional health benefits, but enhanced pleasure. In 1927, for example, he patented a process for making patterned

The Haller Girls at the Berlin Wintergarten, 1926

condoms. The documentation for this patent explains that "the patterned surface can be given any form, such as stripes and geometric shapes, in one or in several colors."

Moreover, the ever-resourceful condom manufacturer wrote on his package inserts: "In addition to standard sizes we also supply a variety of additional widths by request. Let your supplier know about any special requirements, and the supplier will place the appropriate order with us." A boxed notice reminded customers: "Common decency dictates that you not carelessly toss away our prophylactics and packaging after use, or else they will be found lying on streets, city squares, or walkways. Keep our printed matter away from the eyes of minors. It is not intended for them."[9]

By the end of the 1920s, Fromm's products were so popular that beer hall cabarettists and piano-bar comedians in Berlin were incorporating Fromms Act condoms into their routines, singing lines like "Fromms with your girl—give it a whirl," "When the urge grabs you, grab Fromms Act," and "Just like a Fromm—I'm ready to come." Fromm had made it. He did not have to pitch his condoms. Customers read the name and got the picture.

From the Ghetto in Konin to Berlin

JULIUS FROMM OFTEN CLAIMED that he was born in Poznan, Prussia, and that his parents chose the name Julius for him. Neither statement is true. He was actually born—on March 4, 1883—in the small town of Konin, seventy-five miles east of Poznan, in what was then Russia. At his bris, his name was entered into the synagogue register as Israel From. The birth of his father, Baruch, had been recorded in the same register, on October 10, 1854. At that time, Konin had 5,147 inhabitants, 2,006 of them Jews, the others Polish Catholics and German Protestants.[10] In the Middle Ages, the Jews had fled to the East from France, the Rhineland, and Bohemia to escape discrimination and Christian bloodlust. Konin was among the first twelve Polish communities in which Jews were permitted to settle.

The descendants of the people driven from their homelands spoke Yiddish, and most of them lived near the Warta River, in their own quarter surrounding the Tepper Marik (Pot Market). In 1766 the Jewish community completed the construction of a magnificent synagogue, and later added a *beit midrash* as a place of study and prayer. The modest dwellings in this neighborhood were typically made of wood. The unpaved streets turned to mud whenever it rained or the Warta overflowed.

The Jews of Konin set great store by tradition. The men wore beards and, at least on religious holidays, black caftans. The married women wore *sheitls* (wigs). They observed the Sabbath and kept strict kosher households, and the rabbi settled disputes. Contraception was considered a grave sin, tantamount to blood-shed. Even so, strict orthodoxy barely gained a toehold in this small town at the extreme western end of tsarist Russia.

The surviving members of the Fromm family have no infor-mation concerning Baruch Fromm's childhood, background, parents, or other ancestors, but the Poznan Voivodeship (prov-ince) Archives has the Konin synagogue register in its holdings. This book contains a Russian-language entry in the Cyrillic alpha-bet for the wedding of Baruch Fromm and Sara Rifka Riegel, which reads:

In the town of Konin, on the 19th of February/2nd of March 1880, at four after midnight, Rabbi Hirsch Auerbach of Konin entered the building, together with Boruch From, merchant, twenty-five years old, son of the married couple Moschka and Bluma From, residing here in Konin, and Sura Rifka Riegel, maiden, twenty-two years old, daughter of the married couple Sondra and Esther Riegel, residing in the town of Konin, along with the parents of the groom and bride. In the presence of wit-nesses Moschka Buchner, forty-nine years old, and Abraham Bock, forty-three years old, Hirsch Auerbach declared that Boruch From and Sura Rifka had entered into the holy bond of matri-mony. This marriage was preceded by three blessings over the Torah readings before the congregation in the Konin synagogue. The newlyweds declared that their prenuptial contract had been signed in the presence of Serafim Gurski, the notary in Konin, on the 19th of February/2nd of March of this year. A dowry was paid. The parents' consent was declared orally. This act will be signed after it is read aloud by the rabbi, the witnesses, and all others present.

This entry shows that the newlyweds were not from the lowest class of the Konin ghetto, since they were able to afford the services of a notary, and their possessions were valuable enough to warrant a prenuptial agreement. The double wedding date reflects the difference between the Julian calendar—which was still in use by the Russian Orthodox Church—and the Gregorian calendar, in effect in the Polish Catholic western regions.

The synagogue register also contains entries for the births of the Fromms' first three sons. The notation for the second son, Israel (who later went by Julius), reads as follows:

In the town of Konin, on the 1st of March/13th of March 1883, at ten after midnight, Boruch From, merchant, twenty-eight years old, residing here in the town of Konin, appeared in the presence of witnesses Israel-Gersch Parschinski, scribe of the synagogue, thirty-five years old, and Moschka Singerman, member of the community, sixty-three years old, both residing in the town of Konin. From produced an infant of the male gender who was born on the 20th of February/4th of March of the current year at three after midnight here in the town of Konin to his legitimate wife Rifka, née Riegel, twenty-five years old. This infant was named Israel From at his bris. After the document was read aloud, it was signed by us, as witnesses, and by the child's father.[11]

Szlama had been born two and a half years earlier, in late November 1880. Mosziek, Helene, Siegmund, Esther, Sander, and Bernhard followed over the years to come.

Postcard view of the shtetl *in Konin during the tsarist period*

———

Tsarist Russia, of which Konin had been a part since 1815, had no compulsory schooling. Most Jewish boys attended small, private religious schools called *cheder* (Hebrew for "room"). They learned Hebrew from the age of four, and later studied the Bible. They memorized Torah passages and other religious scriptures. A little arithmetic was the only curricular concession to modernity.

Helene Fromm later told her nephews and nieces that her father, Baruch, had owned a large estate in Konin, but this is one of those embellished stories that tend to arise in families who work their way up from rags to riches, and attain community prestige within a generation. In the nineteenth century, there was only a single Jewish landowner in the vicinity of Konin, a man named Kaplan. In 1890 one Jewish doctor and one lawyer had their practices in town. The other Jews worked as blacksmiths, stonemasons, saddlers, tailors, and shoemakers; many were merchants.

Shtetl life had been imposed upon the Jews by society at large, yet to some degree it was also a self-chosen oasis of safety and autonomy. Many progressive-minded young Jews disdained these quarters, regarding them as nothing more than overpopulated places of poverty and sanctimoniousness. The radiant haze of nostalgia settled over shtetls only after their devastation by the Germans.

By the 1880s, the Jews constituted over half of Konin's population. They had great difficulty finding work to keep them afloat, so an increasing number of them moved westward. For many of the Jewish emigrants, the desire for a better and more prosperous life meant relocating to Germany. Baruch and Sara Fromm and their children joined the ranks of Jews heading to Berlin. A later family story had the parents fleeing pogroms in Konin, but this appears unlikely in light of the information contained in Theo Richmond's thorough and affectionate chronicle of this community, *Konin: A Quest*. Richmond's meticulous research reveals that while many of the Christians in Konin—both Catholic Poles and Protestant Germans—were united in their anti-Semitism and ranted about "the dirty Jews," there was no systematic violence here in the late nineteenth century. Notwithstanding their religious and linguistic differences, the people of Konin lived in reasonably peaceful coexistence.

In 1893, the Fromms left their homeland. Baruch looked forward to the prospect of a decent life and better opportunities for his children. The economic vitality of the rapidly expanding city of Berlin became their beacon of hope. A community of Eastern European Jewish immigrants was already well established there, thus paving the way for the fresh start they were seeking. Germany offered the Jewish immigrants a measure of legal security, freedom of movement, and liberty to choose their own profession, all of which seemed idyllic in comparison with tsarist Russia.

———

Mulackstrasse 9, ground floor, was the first German address recorded for Baruch Fromm. It is listed in the 1894 edition of the

Address Book for Berlin and Its Suburbs. The family of seven appears to have shared a single room in this area of Berlin, which was notorious for its criminality. Mulackstrasse runs through the Scheunenviertel area, situated northwest of Alexanderplatz. This quarter, with its dilapidated houses and narrow streets, was the first destination for most Jews who had immigrated from the east. Rents were low. Old buildings just two or three stories high stood adjacent to stables and ramshackle sheds. In many ways, this neighborhood resembled the homelands these newcomers had just left. In the late nineteenth century, investors avoided the area. Elsewhere, they were constructing the five-story tenements that would come to typify Berlin. These buildings were shooting up throughout the city—everywhere, that is, but here.

"Stores with Hebrew signs and the oddest names instantly reveal the foreign nature of the area. In the summer there is a lively bustle of the sort you would find at an open market in Galicia or Poland," wrote the novelist Adolf Sommerfeld in describing the Scheunenviertel. Immigrants like the Fromms were not responsible for giving this neighborhood its bad reputation. The crowd that dragged the area down consisted of "felons and prostitutes and their work-averse hangers-on living here, as parasites of the nonviolent Eastern European Jews." The Mulackritze Pub became a favorite haunt for the Berlin underworld. It attracted criminals, whores, hustlers, alcoholics, and stool pigeons. Two gangs of ex-convicts, Immertreu (ever-devoted) and Felsenfest (solid as a rock), were among the regulars. A small brothel in the attic, furnished with several cots, turned a brisk business.[12]

After a year, the Fromms found a new place to live, just a few hundred yards down the street, at Kleine Rosenthaler Strasse 12. Soon thereafter they moved about a hundred yards south, to Steinstrasse 24, and then to Gormannstrasse 21. Most likely they did not have much in the way of personal belongings to move.

The buildings on Kleine Rosenthaler Strasse and Steinstrasse are long since gone, as is the house at Mulackstrasse 9, which is now the site of a pristine playground. However, Gormannstrasse 21 still conveys a sense of how people lived in the Scheunenviertel at that time. This three-story house with a converted attic has a steep staircase leading upstairs from the courtyard entrance. The staircase is too narrow to accommodate two people at a time. On each floor a dark hallway leads to four small apartments and a shared toilet. When the Fromms moved onto Gormannstrasse, there were twenty-three tenants listed in the address book for this building. The men worked as masons, carriage drivers, sign painters, tailors, glove makers, and waiters.

At some point Baruch Fromm changed his Hebrew first name to Bernhard. His wife, Sara Rifka, became Regina; Szlama, the eldest son, went by Salomon. The second-eldest, Israel, opted for Julius; his sister Esther was now called Else; and Mosziek (Moses) became Max.

Bernhard Fromm found work selling cigarettes. In the address book entry for 1894, he listed himself as a "cigarette dealer," and a year later as a "cigarette manufacturer." This new branch of industry—the cigarette as a cigar for the masses—had been initiated by Eastern European Jewish immigrants. Klara Eschelbacher described the circumstances that resulted in their interest in the cigarette business in her 1920 dissertation "The Eastern European Jewish Immigrant Population of the City of Berlin": "At that time Russian-Polish Jews, who had brought little more than their manual dexterity, tried to earn a living by rolling cigarettes during the day and selling them one by one in cafés at night." The author of this dissertation was seeking to establish the extent to which Eastern European Jews aimed to integrate into mainstream society and advance their position in Berlin, or, in her words, "whether and how Eastern European Jews were able to settle in and adapt here under normal circumstances."

In 1894 the Tobacco Professional Association in Berlin comprised twenty-one cigarette factories with 111 workers, plus approximately seven hundred family businesses making cigarettes for the local market. The Fromms had one of the latter businesses. The tobacco products were made by hand; blending the tobacco and rolling it into the cigarette papers required skill. This line of work lent itself to impoverished immigrants, because it required virtually no start-up capital. Paper that cost twenty pfennigs and tobacco ninety-five pfennigs would yield about a thousand cigarettes.

This cottage industry enabled Jews to observe the Sabbath. But "the greatest benefit," according to Eschelbacher, "was the prospect of autonomy it offered." "With a wife and children pitching in, cigarettes were often rolled until two in the morning. A deft worker with several older children sometimes reached an output of as many as 3,000 cigarettes."[13] Bernhard Fromm began by selling cigarettes for other companies, then manufactured and sold the product himself. Naturally the whole family had to help out.

Bernhard Fromm died on June 18, 1898, at the age of only forty-two, quite possibly as a direct result of working under poor conditions, inhaling tobacco particles, and living in wretched housing.

———

At the time of Bernhard's death, the Fromms had been living in Berlin for five years, and the widow and her children found themselves in desperate straits. The family lacked a breadwinner, but fortunately Gormannstrasse had a cooking school belonging to the Jewish community that supplied inexpensive food to the needy. Moreover, Regina Fromm was in the third trimester of her latest pregnancy. At the end of her rope, she felt she had no choice but to place her youngest sons, Siegmund and Alexander, in the Baruch-Auerbach Orphans Educational Institute at Schönhauser Allee 162. In July 1898, just one month after the death of her husband, she

Fromm family, ca. 1904; standing from left: Max, Else, Siegmund, Helene, Julius; seated from left: Alexander, Regina (mother), Bernhard

gave birth to her sixth son, and named him Bernhard in memory of her deceased husband.

Since his older brother, Salomon, had emigrated to London, and remained there for several years, fifteen-year-old Julius had to take care of his mother and siblings. The family continued making cigarettes at home—for the years 1899 to 1907, "R[egina] Fromm, W[i]d[ow]" was listed in the address book as *Cigarettenmanu*. Later on, Julius became an employee of Josetti Cigarettes, where he quickly worked his way up in the business. A photograph taken circa 1904 shows Regina Fromm with seven of her children in festive outfits and earnest expressions.

When Julius started his own family in 1907, at the age of twenty-four, he and his wife and their newborn son (whom they had named Max, like many assimilationist Jews of the time) moved to the nearby Bötzow area in the Prenzlauer Berg district of Berlin, which had fairly decent Wilhelmine-style tenements.

On left: Salomon Fromm, Julius's older brother, ca. 1907
On right: Helene Fromm, Julius's younger sister, ca. 1910

His mother and younger siblings soon moved into a neighboring apartment. They were now living at Allensteiner Strasse 40. The street has since been renamed Liselotte Hermann Strasse in honor of a communist student executed in 1938. Their neighbors included a postal worker, a jeweler, and a furrier. The Fromms were coming up in the world.

———

Julius's father had lived to the age of forty-two. His mother passed away when she was fifty-two, on July 13, 1911. Their unadorned double tombstone, at the Jewish cemetery in Berlin-Weissensee, carries this inscription: "Here lie our dearly beloved parents. In their unselfish love for their children, they passed away far too soon." Klara Eschelbacher observed that "Eastern European Jews who were willing and able to work, even when they had virtually nothing upon entering the country, were able to save up money relatively quickly by living incredibly frugally." Scrimping and saving opened up new opportunities for "Eastern European Jews ... to carve out better futures for themselves and especially for their children. In pursuit of this goal, they are willing to go hungry and live a miserable life."

Salomon and Julius were now solely responsible for their brothers and sisters. They proved equal to the challenge that lay ahead. Eschelbacher characterized the typical Eastern European Jewish cigarette maker, such as Julius Fromm, as "a quintessential 'entrepreneurial proletariat' [who hoped] with some justification to become a manufacturer some day."[14] As the manual assembly of cigarettes gradually gave way to machine production, Julius Fromm sought an alternative career. "Rolling cigarettes forever wasn't good enough for him anyway," his son Edgar recalled, "so he started taking evening courses in chemistry in 1912—especially in rubber chemistry—and hit upon the idea of making condoms."

Max, Julius's eldest son, with wooden hoop and playmates, in the Bötzow section of Berlin–Prenzlauer Berg, ca. 1915

Two years later, he founded a one-man company: Israel Fromm, Manufacturing and Sales Company for Perfumes and Rubber Goods. He rented a store at Lippehner Strasse 23, which today bears the name of Käthe Niederkirchner, a communist who was shot at the Ravensbrück concentration camp in 1944. From this point on, Fromm considered himself a merchant. In 1914 his business was outfitted with a telephone ("Telephone Exchange: Königstadt 431"). He set up an account at Dresdner Bank, and before long he also had a telegram address ("Frommsact Berlin"). The classified directory carried a listing for his "seamless rubber products," which in 1915 he expanded to read: "rubber products and perfume factory." In 1916 a highlighted entry announced: "I. Fromm, Special Manufacturing of Rubber Products. Fromms Act."

Giacomo Casanova had taken to using condoms back in the eighteenth century; in his memoirs he referred to them as "English riding coats." The early condoms, generally made of sheep intestine and fish bladder, were far from satisfactory. They were used primarily by wealthy people who wanted protection against syphilis, then incurable. These condoms offered only limited protection against infection and interfered with lovemaking so exasperatingly that the Marquise de Sévigné disparaged them as "armor against pleasure, and a cobweb against danger." A set of instructions issued by the Social Democratic Party public health spokesman Alfred Grotjahn in the 1920s makes it clear that contraceptives made of animal innards left a lot to be desired in their reliability and ease of use: "The condom, pulled over the penis, has to be moistened with water, after which it fits snugly. For added peace of mind, a second condom is pulled over it, and its outer side is lubricated with some fat. After sexual intercourse the condom can be washed out and reused, provided there are no holes."[15]

The technical prerequisite for modern condoms was the rubber vulcanization process that Charles Goodyear had invented in

1839. When the sap of the rubber tree (*Hevea brasiliensis*) is formed into rubber, then treated with sulfur and heated to a high temperature, it forms a mass that is both elastic and durable. Soon the rubber produced in this manner was being made into raincoats and shoes. The major product was, of course, tires. In the United States, condoms were made this way as well, and "rubber" became a synonym for condom. But these early condoms were like bicycle inner tubes with bulging seams, which understandably limited their popularity and sales. A special dipping method that would produce seamless and sheer condoms inexpensively was eventually developed, and sales took off. Engineers at Goodyear appear to have begun manufacturing the first condoms with this method in 1901, but it took quite a while for the product to attain industrial maturity.

Julius Fromm was the one to accomplish this in Germany. A child of a penniless immigrant family, he put the right product on the market at the right time and in the right place. In 1995 his son Edgar summed up his path to success: "Shortly before World War I, my father tried to make reputable brand-name merchandise out of a product that had been regarded as shoddy and virtually taboo. It was designed to provide protection against virulent sexually transmitted diseases and at the same time aid in family planning. He succeeded perfectly. Julius Fromm was endowed with a fabulous knack for business."

THE WORLD'S FIRST BRAND-NAME CONDOMS

IN LATE 1906, Julius and his fiancée, Selma Lieders, the daughter of a shoemaker, took a rather hurried trip to London. They got
married there on December 27. The twenty-three-year-old listed
his profession as "cigarette maker" and his bride's as "cap maker."
Julius's brother Salomon was the best man. Salomon had emigrated to the British capital some time earlier—in part as protest
against his mother's religious strictness. Now going by the name
Sally, he worked in the cigarette business and also became editor
of a Yiddish-language newspaper.

The crucial factor in Julius's decision to get married far from
home was Selma's pregnancy. Their son Max was born in Berlin
just four months after the marriage ceremony. Five years later,
they had a second child, Herbert, after which a full seven years
passed until Edgar was born in 1919. Although Julius's parents
do not appear to have practiced birth control, contraception was
evidently of personal as well as professional interest to Julius
Fromm.

"He did not suffer fools gladly," says the London textile agent Raymond Fromm about his grandfather Julius. Julius Fromm was purposeful and meticulous, and he expected the same level of professionalism and devotion from his staff. If people let him down, he could become quite merciless.

Julius Fromm comes across as an enormously diligent man whose world revolved around work and his company. In the few remaining photographs of Fromm, he seems serious and focused even at family gatherings. He read and spoke fluent Hebrew, but his education was otherwise minimal. In Berlin he had briefly attended the Eighth Community Elementary School. He acquired on his own the chemical and business skills he needed to establish his company, and he had no capital to invest. This modest foundation was all he had to build on when he went into business in 1914, the year the Great War began. The war increased the demand for condoms. Fromm hired several workers, and the business soon outgrew his shop-plus-apartment in the Bötzow area of Berlin. He then rented a new set of rooms in one of the standard industrial complexes at Elisabethstrasse 28/29, near the Spree River in the Berlin-Mitte district, where he manufactured

Julius Fromm's identity card photograph, 1918

his condoms from 1917 to 1922. The adjoining businesses in-cluded a corset factory, a children's clothing maker named Cohn-Meiser, and Friedländer & Grunwald, a manufacturer of feather dusters.

As the "widely known, well-established Fromms Act hygienic and surgical rubber goods" grew ever more popular, Fromm added more rooms at Landsberger Strasse 73, directly at Alexanderplatz. He proudly described his factory rooms, which were still modest in size at that time, as "workplaces adapted to the modern large firm." He invited "prospective buyers in the rubber goods trade" to have a look at his "large permanent showcase."[16] To meet the growing demand, he occasionally produced additional inventory at Hatu Rubber Works in Erfurt.

It was in 1916 that the young entrepreneur chose the name "Fromms Act" for his company. Although there is no record of how he came to include the English spelling of the word "Act" in the company name, it seems likely that he got the idea from his older brother, Salomon, who had developed an eye for the inter-national market while in London.

Julius Fromm tended to rely on Salomon for business advice. The two of them may have figured that "Fromms Act" sounded appealing, even a tad risqué, and that the cosmopolitan connota-tion would spark sales. In both German and English, the word "act" (*Akt* in German) means "action" as well as an "act" of a the-atrical or sexual nature, and in German it also refers to the painted nude, and thus to the naked body. Moreover, the German word suggests the seriousness of a near-homonym, *Akte* (dossier), and sounds like an abbreviation of *Aktiengesellschaft* (corporation), thereby conveying the impression of a well-established, prosper-ous enterprise. In reality, of course, Fromm was running a humble operation in Berlin, but in no time at all, Fromms Act became such a household name that when Ruth Fromm was a teenager,

One of the first advertisements in the trade journal
Der Drogenhändler, 1917

she turned bright red with embarrassment when asked about her uncle's company.

For the packaging, Fromm chose small striped cardboard boxes in his favorite colors, green and purple. Each box contained three condoms. At a price of seventy-two pfennigs per box, Fromm's condoms were not inexpensive, but they offered better value and quality than any of his competitors' products. "Attaching our own name to this article," Edgar explained, "was my father's bright idea." It was a bold move for Fromm literally to put his name on the line for a product whose failure could be devastating. He inserted his full name, Julius Fromm, into the sweeping upstroke of the A in "Act," which curled back onto the word "Fromms."

Until that time, customers had only the foggiest notion of where their condoms had originated, and the quality of these condoms was abysmal. To get around having to provide warranties for these sought-after commodities, Fromm's competitors used an ever-changing array of fancy names—such as Ramses, Mikado, Uncle Sam, Dingsda, Souvenir, Viola, and Venus—to market their condoms in Germany. This practice continued into

Max, Julius, Herbert, and Selma Fromm,
ca. 1916

the 1920s. The British company London Rubber did not introduce the brand name Durex—today the global leader—until 1929.

Initially Fromm also had to contend with serious quality issues.
There were "large numbers of rejects," one worker recalled after
the war, "and Herr Fromm quite often took whole sackfuls of
them, called us in, and asked, 'Would you want to buy these from
me?'" The production process was soon refined, and a combination of relatively high retail prices, a marked increase in demand, and a switch to piecework wages soon resulted in sizable
profits.

Glass cylinders served as molds for the condoms. They were
mounted on carrier frames, then dipped into a vat containing a

rubber solution liquefied with gasoline, benzene, and carbon tet-rachloride. Experiments made it clear to Fromm that "Ceylon rubber is best suited to the manufacture of Fromms products." After two dippings, a thin rubber skin adhered to the cylinders. This skin was then brushed to roll the open side into a bulging rim. Next, the condoms were vulcanized in special ovens using sulfur vapors. The key factors in making the little rubber skins sturdy yet elastic, and durable enough to be warehoused, were strictly calibrated ingredients, temperature, and timing. All this required, as Fromm said, "a very well-trained staff."

The condoms were dusted with a lubricant to give them a "vel-vety surface," then rolled off the glass cylinders, tested, inverted, and packaged. Using the technical principles still employed today, Fromm also manufactured surgical finger cots, rubber gloves, pacifiers, and nipples for baby bottles.

From the outset, he insisted on quality. In 1917 Fromm launched the advertising slogan "We guarantee our products—exchanges accepted at any time."[17] After a few years, he introduced a three-step inspection process. First, "each item, one by one [was] inflated with compressed air." The condoms that passed this round then underwent a "second, even more rigorous test" and then a third in the rolling room, where "the tips of the items that proved sat-isfactory in the earlier tests are inflated to recheck their imper-meability, sheerness, elasticity, and durability."

According to a report by Magnus Hirschfeld, quality control was the reason Fromms products had attained an "international reputation": "with unreliable brands, these tests are not rigorous or comprehensive. . . . A good company is vigilant in rejecting all items that fall short of its high standards. One way to achieve this is to pay the testers according to the number of flawed items iden-tified, which is the method used at Fromms Act."

In 1931 Julius Fromm posted advertisements announcing

"Fromms Act—Information" on advertising pillars in "numerous cities." The text read:

> Buy our popular select brand, Fromms Act, exclusively at these specialty stores: apothecaries, drugstores, rubber goods stores, first-aid shops, perfumeries, and barbershops. There you will be assured of purchasing *fresh merchandise* that has been properly stored and carefully handled. [There] you will obtain our select brand, Fromms Act, in our *original packaging* with *our inspection numbers*. These inspection numbers enable us to ensure that only *fresh merchandise* is sold. The proprietors at the specialty stores are aware of their responsibility to the public and understand the significance of our inspection numbers. If you should happen to be offered our select brand in packaging where the inspection numbers have been *scratched off* or *erased*, do not accept these items. This is for your own good! . . . Always make a point of demanding the genuine select brand, Fromms Act, so that you will not be disappointed.[18]

———

In 1919 Julius Fromm was able to buy a villa in Nikolassee for 95,000 Reichsmarks. The property was located near the Schlachtensee in an upscale section of Zehlendorf, a suburb in southwest Berlin, which is why its location is listed variously as Nikolassee, Zehlendorf, and Schlachtensee. Now the family of five could spread out in the villa's eight rooms over two stories. There was also a maid's room in the attic, a spacious kitchen, and a chauffeur's apartment in the basement. The up-and-coming condom manufacturer felt that he could finally consider himself a German, and legal confirmation of his naturalization soon followed.

———

Julius Fromm had applied for Prussian citizenship back in September 1914. His stated reasons for wishing to become a German

Left to right: Julius Fromm's three sons, Max, Edgar, and Herbert, with an unknown business associate of their father's, in the garden of the family's villa in Berlin-Schlachtensee, ca. 1922

citizen are provided on his application form: "I came to Berlin as a very young child. The German language was not unfamiliar to me because my parents always spoke German, and in no time at all I had forgotten my previous place of residence. I am ardently devoted to my second homeland, and for me, a return to Russia would be worse than death." The applicant indicated that his annual income fell between 3,000 and 3,500 marks, and that his assets came to 8,000 marks. Fromm explained that he did not want to be considered a Russian on account of the war; "enemy aliens" had to report to the police precinct on a regular basis: "I can no longer bear to carry around this stigma, and I would like to spare my children the disgrace of finding themselves in the same situation."

He was not overly eager to join the war effort, however: "Unfortunately I cannot carry out my wish to fight in the war against Russia as a volunteer, because my health has been problematic for some time. It would be my greatest source of pride, though, if I should someday have the privilege of seeing my two sons as strapping Prussian soldiers." Of course at this point they were still children, ages seven and three, and their physical appearance did not mark them as outsiders. Max, the older of the two, had blond hair. Indeed, Julius's own identity card, issued in 1918, listed his hair as blond, and his eyes as grayish blue.

Even so, the Royal Police President of Berlin rejected the application. His official statement read: "Politically, Fromm is beyond reproach. Our misgivings about his naturalization are based on the fact that he has neither a secure livelihood nor assets to his name." In a handwritten note in the margin, an administrator in the aliens' division put the group's objections more bluntly: "Russian Jew without a secure livelihood, who cannot or will not serve in the military." In any event, he was exempted from the tiresome duty of reporting regularly to the police as a "Russian."

In 1919, Fromm again applied for citizenship, this time with a lawyer at his side. He now had "a well-established business," had proved to be "a good taxpayer," and underscored his sincere German loyalty during the war. He had become a "member of several charitable organizations for soldiers and veterans . . . donating money to the Red Cross on many occasions, and collecting gold coins for the patriotic cause." In the accompanying application, Fromm moved back the date of his family's immigration by three years, most likely to make it appear that he had spent more time attending school in Berlin. As a precaution, he added: "I am unable to provide the exact date." Apart from that, he filled out the form truthfully, stating: "I have not been supported by public welfare, I am a homeowner, and I support myself and my family as a self-sufficient businessman. My family's annual income is about 25,000 marks." In today's terms, that would be about 250,000 euros.

Fromm's business associates provided written character references. The Berlin branch manager of the Metzeler Rubber Factory stated, "I have come to know Mr. Fromm as a competent, prudent, and honest businessman, and I value his good patriotic attitude in particular, even though I know that he is a foreigner." The business partners at Hatu Rubber Works in Erfurt supported him in similar language in 1920 and attested "that he promises to become a good German citizen." The police voted in favor of naturalization and composed this statement: "The applicant has a rubber goods business at Lippehnerstrasse 23 and employs 12 people there. Moreover, he is the joint owner of an optician's shop at Alexanderstrasse 71, with a staff of 6. On October 1 [1919], he moved his place of residence to Schlachtensee,

Son Herbert in Julius Fromm's automobile, ca. 1930

Rolandstrasse 4, where he lives in a single-family dwelling with 10 rooms. His economic situation is thoroughly in order."

In July 1920, the chief administrative officer in Potsdam issued Fromm a certificate of naturalization. He was the first of his siblings to acquire German citizenship. This certificate read: "With the issuance of this document, the merchant Israel Fromm in Zehlendorf-West, born on March 4/February 20, 1893 in Konin (Russia), and his wife and children have acquired Prussian citizenship and have hence become German nationals." Three years later, the district court of Berlin-Lichterfelde authorized him "to go by the first name 'Julius' instead of his original first name Israel."[19]

———

In February 1922, Julius Fromm bought a larger lot for his business in the quiet suburb of Friedrichshagen at the extreme eastern end of Berlin. He wanted to expand production as quickly as possible, but lacking sufficient capital of his own, he mortgaged his residence to the allowable limit. Benefiting from the tremendous inflation in Germany, he was able to pay off his debt-secured mortgage in the amount of 200,000 Reichsmarks a mere ten months later.[20]

He submitted an application to renovate a small existing factory building and to construct a factory workroom in Friedrichshagen, thus adding a second location to the business. However, the site was zoned as Construction Category F, for which this standard regulation applied: "Factories that create a disturbance are forbidden in this location." Despite this regulation, the building control authority issued him a building permit, provided certain conditions were met. This authority evidently gave precedence to potential economic benefits over safeguarding the rights of neighbors. The Industry Supervisory Board of Treptow-Köpenick ruled: "The gases and steam created by the vulcanization of rubber products have to be extracted and rendered harmless in a suitable manner at the point of origin. Under no circumstances can these processes create a nuisance for the workers or the neighbors." Enforcement of this regulation was only partly successful in defusing conflicts, however. Right from the start, Fromm was besieged with complaints from the neighbors. Solutions of natural rubber in a petroleum solvent posed an ongoing fire hazard. In May 1926, a local fire department reported: "When the fire broke out, three factory workers sustained slight injuries—burns and lacerations. They were treated by the Friedrichshagen volunteer first-aid crew and released."[21]

Fromm commissioned the architects Arthur Korn and Siegfried Weitzmann, who subscribed to the Neue Sachlichkeit (New

Fromm had a series of slides made for promotional purposes in 1935. The thirty-seven extant photographs document work routines in his factory— such as the condom testing displayed here

Objectivity) style of architecture, to design the new factory floor and office wing (parts of which are still standing today). Now the neighbors complained not only about the noise and fumes but also about the aesthetics of the new building, which clashed with their gabled homes. A letter to the editor in a local newspaper, the *Niederbarnimer Zeitung*, argued that "the flat roof [of the new building is] an architectural impossibility." Moreover, the angry neighbor who sent this letter warned "the highest authorities" that he and other established members of the community would "not put up with any further defacement of this area by buildings of this kind."

"Complaints about the stench and racket emanating from the rubber factory," reported the local paper in September 1928, "have not ceased since the day the factory began its operations." The article went on to claim that adjacent properties were "subjected day and night to such powerful droning and thudding from the rolling mills and mixers as well as from the boiler plants and their steam exhaust pipes that heavy pieces of furniture in the neighbors' rooms sometimes start shaking." As a result, the residents were "robbed of sleep and unable to focus on their work."

"Our factory," Fromm retorted in the local newspaper, "employs the latest technology to prevent unpleasant odors and disturbing sounds to the greatest extent possible, and we have spared no expense in making our company a model company."[22]

Fromm himself may have been quite unpopular with his neighbors, but the opposite was true of his leading product. In 1926 Fromms Act manufactured 24 million condoms. Two years later, the business had agencies in Bremen, Breslau, Cologne, Danzig (today Gdansk in Poland), Düsseldorf, Essen, Frankfurt, Hamburg, Hanover, Kiel, Königsberg (today Kaliningrad in Russia), Leipzig, Munich, Rostock, and Würzburg. Exports were handled by branches in Antwerp, Constantinople, Czernowitz (today

Chernivtsi in Ukraine), The Hague, Kattowitz (today Katowice in Poland), London, Riga, Reykjavík, Auckland, Budapest, and Zurich. By 1931 Fromms Act had undergone a major expansion. With added production plants in Köpenick and Danzig, the company produced more than 50 million condoms that year.

Even the world economic crisis did not cause a slump in sales at Fromms Act. "Business is brisk even now," the German Credit Bureau ascertained in February 1933, about the company and about Fromm himself. "Sales are in the millions. The company's products are well established. : . . Our sources describe Fromm as an extremely competent and ambitious businessman who has worked his way up over the years to a position of wealth. We are aware of nothing negative of any sort."[23]

Julius Fromm ate lunch with his staff in the cafeteria, and considered hard work the key to success. Every afternoon he rested on his office couch—for exactly twenty minutes. His motto was "Ever onward!"

4·

"We Have Become Germans"—An Illusion

JULIUS FROMM'S SEVEN SIBLINGS were no match for their fabulously successful brother, but they too built up small businesses and earned respectable livelihoods. Only Max (whose name was originally Mosziek) continued to lean on the family for financial support. He eked out a living as a self-employed women's tailor, and died in 1930 at the age of forty-five.

When Salomon returned to Berlin from London in 1912, he married, and opened an optician's shop at Siegmundshof in the Tiergarten area of the city. Alexander, who had borrowed money from his brother Julius to set up an optical company on Alexanderstrasse, moved his shop to Memhardstrasse in 1925. Helene took up the same line of work as her two brothers, and opened her store right in the center of the city, at the Spittelmarkt.

Siegmund Fromm and his brother-in-law Willy Brandenburg (his sister Else's husband) tried their hand at a business similar to the one Julius was running. Their company, which was registered in June 1921 as Fromm & Brandenburg, produced soaps, perfumes, and creams. Bernhard Fromm, the youngest brother, later joined them. Bernhard, Siegmund, and Willy each owned one-third of Fromms Cosmetics Associates. They later gave the company an English name, Fromm Brothers, to appeal to an international market.

The company's signature cream, Fromms Skin Food, which was used to treat rough, dry, and sunburned skin, became a big moneymaker. Many barbershops and drugstores in Berlin had signs with the advertising jingle "Fromms Act for the bride, Fromms Skin Food for the hide."

The cosmetics business and the optician's shops yielded handsome profits. The Fromms were not quite in the lap of luxury, but they lived very comfortably, and had the means to take a summer vacation, which was somewhat out of the ordinary in

Salomon Fromm's optician's shop in Berlin-Tiergarten, ca. 1930

the 1920s. They and their families lived in the upscale western section of Berlin. On Sundays the family typically gathered in the large garden of Julius's villa or went for a stroll in the Tiergarten park.

The immigrants of Julius's generation were not especially well educated—how could they be?—but their children were expected to learn, learn, and learn some more. They studied the piano or some other instrument, and graduated from high school if at all possible. Salomon began to teach English to his daughter Ruth when she was only three years old. He was exasperated to no end by her older brother Berthold's limited aptitude.

The Fromm siblings, who were the first generation of the family to grow up in Germany, cast aside the "religious fixation" of their parents. Ruth reports that when the school administration expelled her from the Königstädtisches Gymnasium in 1936 because she was Jewish, the local Jewish high school refused to accept her because her upbringing had not been sufficiently religious. Left with no choice but to attend the Jewish school on Grosse Hamburger Strasse, a school she considered "dreadful," she balked: "What was I doing learning Hebrew all of a sudden? And all that religion! I didn't know a word of Yiddish, and there I was with a bunch of ghetto children." Even so, the new surroundings rubbed off on her, and no sooner did she use Yiddish expressions at home than all hell broke loose: "Not because they were afraid of the Nazis, but because such uneducated blather was not to enter their home. After all, we were now German!" In all the brouhaha about this "Jewish nonsense," Ruth quit school altogether and began an apprenticeship at Rosenbaum Textile Company, but her stay there was similarly short-lived, since she emigrated to England in 1939. There she became a domestic servant and later an assistant medical technician. Briefly, she returned home and served as a translator for the American armed forces stationed in postwar Germany. More than three decades after she had been robbed of her chance for an education in Germany, Ruth Fromm was awarded a master of social sciences degree at Bryn Mawr College in 1968, and later underwent additional training in child psychology and psychiatry. These days she attends synagogue from time to time: "I meet people there who share similar memories, which makes me feel close to my family."

"My father was religious," Edgar Fromm remarked about Julius, "but there was not much discussion about it at home." They belonged to the Jewish community on Fasanenstrasse and observed the holidays. Julius advised his sons to marry Jewish women because a mixed marriage would make it more difficult to raise children in the Jewish faith. Julius Fromm's siblings felt the same way. Elsbeth Kuntze, wife of his younger brother Siegmund, was raised as a Christian, but converted to Judaism before the wedding.

On the left: Salomon, Berthold, and Elvira Fromm, ca. 1917
On the right: Ruth Fromm, daughter of Salomon and Elvira

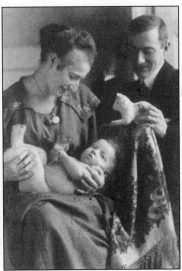

On left: Helene Fromm with unidentified companion, ca. 1915
On right: Else and Willy Brandenburg with their son Bruno, born 1918

"An authoritarian man with a liberal bent" and "a gentle patriarch" are two phrases Edgar Fromm used to describe his father. He was a man of few words, but when he did speak, he was forceful. His circle of friends included both Jews and non-Jews. He was well-regarded in Berlin, but he did not spend much time socializing. The condom manufacturer had both a commanding personality and a progressive outlook. Julius Fromm believed in making condoms a practical means of family planning.

In many respects, the Fromm household was quite permissive—as long as the sons complied with the wishes of the family's "gentle patriarch." But the third immigrant generation, the first to be born in Germany, did not simply do what it was told, as one episode related by Edgar about his eldest brother's choice of profession illustrates.

Max was the most intellectual of the children. After he graduated from Grunewald High School at the age of seventeen, our father said, "So now you're joining the company."

"I don't want to spend my entire life sitting around with the same people from nine to five," Max replied, "I want to become an actor." He was given a clipped reply:

"I will not support that."

The son defiantly headed straight to the renowned theater director Max Reinhardt for an audition, which proved a success.

"You can enroll in the drama school."

"That would be nice, but I have no money," Max replied.

"What? You, the son of Julius Fromm, have no money?" Reinhardt wondered.

"My father said he would not pay for this."

"Then tell him that I have offered you a scholarship and you won't have to pay anything." Our father relented, provided that his son would prove to be an "accomplished actor."

On left: Else Brandenburg, Julius Fromm's younger sister, ca. 1918
On right: Julius Fromm's sister Helene Fromm, ca. 1925

Max could not be swayed from his resolve to pursue a career in acting. He attended Reinhardt's famous drama school from 1928 to 1930, and Julius Fromm brought his younger son Herbert into the business as an apprentice, although Herbert had just finished middle school. Ever true to form, Julius put his son through his paces, making sure that he was assigned the most difficult and unpleasant tasks.

Before long, Max made his theatrical debut, appearing onstage with Max Pallenberg and Fritzi Massary. He also performed in Berlin's leading cabaret, the Kabarett der Komiker (Cabaret of Comedians), which was established in 1924. The cabaret theater, which had seating for eight hundred, featured a stellar array of artists that included Claire Waldoff, Curt Bois, Ernst Busch, Karl Valentin, and the Comedian Harmonists. Friedrich Hollaender, the renowned composer and pianist, who wrote music for the cabaret, took Max Fromm under his wing, and he was soon offered modest roles in film and the theater, including work with Bertolt Brecht. Julius was impressed by his success. Max acted in a series

Fromm family with friends in the garden of the villa, ca. 1928

of entertaining movies produced by UFA, Germany's largest film company: *Eine Freundin so goldig wie du* (A Girlfriend as Sweet as You), *Der Kongress tanzt* (Congress Dances), and *Eine Tür geht auf* (A Door Opens). However, his performances in the Kabarett der Komiker, which was founded by three Jews, drew a dangerous kind of attention to him, since the skits heaped scorn on the National Socialists.

In the spring of 1933, Julius Fromm received a confidential warning that Max was on a Nazi storm trooper black list. His exasperation knew no bounds; hadn't he impressed on his son time and again that associations with a political cabaret and with left-wing, or even communist, friends would someday land him in hot water? Now a new danger loomed. Julius gave Max a large sum of money and urged him to leave Germany immediately.

Max Fromm, who had just turned twenty-seven, said good-bye to a few friends and boarded a train to Amsterdam the very

The actor Max Fromm, ca. 1930

same evening. He hid the money behind a bathroom mirror in the train and brought it safely over the border. He stayed in the Netherlands for three months, then traveled on to Paris, where his fiancée, Paulette Fromm (a distant relative), was awaiting him.

Max spent the summer of 1933 at Hotel Charleston in Montmartre. For a while he shared a room with the actor Peter Lorre, born László Löwenstein. The two had known each other in Berlin. According to Max's brother Edgar, Lorre asked Max one day whether he could lend him a hundred francs to spend the night at the Ritz. "Are you crazy?" Max replied. "No, I'm not crazy," said Lorre. "Alfred Hitchcock is staying there and in the morning I want to come downstairs when he's eating breakfast and announce to him: 'I am Peter Lorre, who played the murderer in Fritz Lang's M. I'm sure you can put me to good use.'"

The rest is history, of course. Hitchcock said little, but did ask for Peter Lorre's telephone number. At first, nothing came of the encounter, but four weeks later, Lorre got a call from Hitchcock's secretary, and went for an audition. He got a principal role in *The Man Who Knew Too Much*, and went on to play unforgettable characters in two films with Humphrey Bogart: *Casablanca* and *The Maltese Falcon*.

Max did not become as well known. He spoke French fluently, but with a German accent. Lorre called him up ecstatically from Hollywood: "Come over here; the Americans don't really mind an accent." But Max was devoted to Paulette, who did not want to leave France or be separated from her widowed mother, so he performed in German-language antifascist cabarets in Paris with Anna Seghers and other émigrés. Paulette and Max supplemented their income by dubbing films.

They married in April 1937. Julius and Selma Fromm came over from Berlin. As a wedding gift they brought a gadget called a View-Master, which contained a rotating disk with thirty-seven little black-and-white images of the new factory in Köpenick. This series of images had been shot in the mid-1930s, and survived the war intact in various attics in Paris. These photographs are the most significant remaining pictorial documents of Fromms Act.

The New Factory: Transparency for Those in the Know

TODAY, FRIEDRICHSHAGENER STRASSE IN KÖPENICK has come to exemplify the demise of industrial Berlin. Shopping centers have replaced the factories that once manufactured products for companies with branches throughout the world. Across from the crumbling cement buildings of the State-Owned Cable Works of Köpenick (the former C. J. Vogel Telegraph Cable Factory), there is now a Kaufland Supermarket and a Toom Home Improvement Center. The big parking lot fills up early in the morning, when senior citizens from the nearby Salvador Allende housing development go shopping. Only one of the locals—a retired truck driver born in 1920—can still recall the street's industrial past, when Kodak and Fromms Rubber Factory were located on the spot where the supermarket stands today, until the end of the war.

Fromms Rubber Factory was built in 1929/30. The site in Friedrichshagen had reached the limit of its production capacity, and the company's profits now allowed for greater capital expenditures. Fromm bought a piece of real estate, measuring over 170,000 square feet, at Friedrichshagener Strasse 38/39 in the Köpenick district of Berlin, near the older site, and again hired the architects Arthur Korn and Siegfried Weitzmann for the project.

Korn and Weitzmann had already renovated Fromm's villa on Rolandstrasse in Schlachtensee, drawn up plans for the factory building annexes in Friedrichshagen, and designed the optician's shops for Julius's brothers Salomon and Alexander. They had been partners since 1922. Korn was responsible primarily for the creative aspect of their work, and Weitzmann was in charge of structural engineering, finances, and construction.

For the new Fromms factory in Köpenick, they erected a three-story administration building facing the street. Its bright red steel construction in a grid pattern measuring 23 by 23 feet was a prominent architectural feature. A covered walkway 475 feet long and 13 feet wide opened up the site, connected the offices with three production halls, and formed the backbone of the whole plant.

Most of the workrooms had full-length glass facades, and glass walls separating the individual rooms created a sense of airiness. In 1931 the architectural magazine *Bauwelt* featured a story about the plant as a prototype of the modern factory: "The design heavily emphasizes objectivity, and the construction makes ample use of the architects' materials of choice: steel, concrete, and glass." The administration building and the production halls were equipped with a climate-control system (which was then called a "ventilation system") that kept "the humidity and the temperature of the rooms at a constant level in summer and winter."[24] The building incorporated the working hypotheses that Ludwig Mies van der Rohe had set forth in 1923: "The office building is a place of work, of organization, of clarity, and of economy. . . . Maximal effect with minimal expenditure of means. The materials are concrete, iron, glass. Reinforced concrete buildings are by nature skeletal buildings. No gingerbread or turrets. Load-bearing girder construction and non-bearing walls. This is skin and bones construction."

Korn and Weitzmann created their magnum opus in Köpenick. Afterward they planned to construct an elegant glass office building on Friedrichstrasse in Berlin-Mitte as a showpiece for Fromms Act. They were unable to realize this project. In 1934, the newly established Reich Chamber for the Fine Arts denied them admission—because they were Jews—effectively barring them from practicing their profession.

While Korn was working on the condom factory design, he published a book bearing the simple title *Glas* (published in English as *Glass in Modern Architecture*). The use of glass was the theoretical basis for the Fromms Act building. Glass had traditionally been considered only a "secondary" material, but Korn advanced the opinion that an "independent skin of glass" could be made, which would open up the view to "the interior, the spaces in depth,

The factory on Friedrichshagener Strasse in Berlin-Köpenick, 1931

and the structural frame that delineates them." The distinction between wall and window would dissolve, since "the wall is this window itself, or, in other words, this wall is itself the window." This dissolution of the exterior boundary of a building is mirrored in an interior innovation: "The interior dividing walls are reduced to glass walls and configured in many different forms."[25] The slides of the Köpenick factory document that at Fromms Act, even the two managing directors worked in a glassed-in cube.

With evident pride, Julius Fromm guided guests and architectural enthusiasts through his factory, which was "impressive," "unique," and constructed "according to the principles of functionality and a healthy work environment." "An abundance of light" would "suffuse" the production and administration wings, making it possible (as Julius Fromm was firmly convinced) "to fill the factory and office workers with pleasure in carrying out their duties."

The aesthetically ambitious functionality and the minimalism of the surrounding outer shell, which Korn called "barely perceptible," was a fitting counterpart to the main product manufactured here. To keep the boundary between inside and outside to an absolute minimum, a Fromm condom could not weigh more than 0.053 ounces. As a result, "a very thin skin" was fashioned, "so translucent" that the protective material was "barely perceptible to the naked eye."[26] Korn's book described his architecture in similar terms: the "disappearance of the outside wall" and the use of glass yielded a "great membrane, full of mystery, delicate yet tough . . . heightening the effect through the occasional glimpses of the load-bearing supports in its interior."

———

In the 1920s, Arthur Korn and Siegfried Weitzmann were part of an avant-garde movement that set trends throughout the world. Korn was born in 1891 in Breslau; his father was a businessman who sold machines, and his mother was a painter. Korn grew up in Berlin. After completing an apprenticeship in carpentry, he graduated from the Royal School of Applied Arts in Berlin. He learned the basics of architecture on his own and by working as an assistant in various offices. In 1914 he was hired by the office of urban planning in Berlin. Korn was intrigued by Herwarth Walden's journal, *Der Sturm*, and by his gallery, where the works of Chagall, Klee, and Kandinsky were displayed, along with early designs by future masters of the Bauhaus.

In July 1914, he volunteered for the Fifth Grenadier Guards Regiment. Decorated with the Iron Cross, he returned to Berlin in 1918. A year later, the architect Erich Mendelsohn invited Korn to become his partner. Together they designed a forty-two-unit housing development in Luckenwalde, near Berlin. "But after six months of working together, we couldn't put up with each other any longer," Korn wrote in a brief autobiographical sketch. Times

Boardroom and switchboard at the Köpenick plant, ca. 1935

were hard for creative young architects, so he turned to interiors and store fixtures, which allowed him ample time for discussion and theorizing.

His manifesto, *Analytical and Utopian Architecture* (1923), shows how profoundly his early theories were shaped by expressionism: "Architecture is a passionate act of love. Writhing. Circling. Pressing down and leaping up. Symbol. Beacons." He insisted "that trenchant analytical construction and the utopia born in the realm of the unconscious intersect in one point."

Just as Korn was publishing his manifesto, the first major commission of his career came his way. A banker named Goldstein hired him to build a fifty-room villa in Berlin-Charlottenburg. Since money was no object, Korn and Weitzmann, who had become partners in 1922, were able to hire the sculptor Rudolf Belling to design several fountains and a water mobile. Richard Neutra added a stylish swimming pool. On the weekends, strollers and architec-

On left: Rolling of rubber blocks, ca. 1935
On right: Dipping room with frames holding glass mandrels
for condoms, ca. 1935

ture buffs gathered in front of the villa and discussed its unusual aesthetics; Walter Gropius included photographs in his *Bauhaus Book No. 1: International Architecture.* Hans Poelzig raved about their work, and proclaimed them two of "the most interesting young modern architects."

Korn and Weitzmann, like several of their fellow architects, worked primarily for middle-class Jewish clients. Since these clients were not steeped in Christian-German traditions, they were able to understand and embrace modern architecture as an expression of social and technical progress. "We had a relatively free hand in creating our designs," said Korn. "We experimented like crazy and were profoundly influenced by the experiments of others." He considered himself an exponent of New Objectivity, which he described as an attempt "to establish boundless beauty in ordinary objects in an appropriate art form." In doing so, he

*Korn and Weitzmann design
for a Fromms Act office building
on Friedrichstrasse, ca. 1929*

sought to "consecrate" ordinary life and "produce architecture that was as highly disciplined as it was adaptable to circumstances." Whatever their political and aesthetic differences, Korn wrote, the members of this group considered themselves "part of a unified force."

Korn regarded the Dutch De Stijl group and the Russian Constructivists (whose slogan was "Art for the people") as kindred spirits who viewed architecture and urban planning within a social and economic context. From his point of view, the revolutions in Russia and Germany in 1917 and 1918 provided "a stream of new ideas" for architecture. "Collective labor," he declared, "is the true key to progress." In 1929, just when the nouveau riche capitalist Fromm was presenting him with his most important commission, Korn founded the Collective for Socialist Construction. This group, which consisted of predominantly radical left-wing students of architecture, designed a blueprint for Berlin called "The City as

On left: Siegfried Weitzmann, ca. 1950
On right: Arthur Korn, ca. 1930

Hotel and Factory," and during the German construction trade show in Berlin organized a counterevent dubbed the Proletarian Construction Exhibition.[27]

Korn made his first trip to London with Walter Gropius in 1934 to attend the International Congress of Modern Architecture (CIAM). He then worked in Zagreb for two years before settling down in England, where he devoted himself to his second passion, urban planning. He began teaching at the Oxford School of Architecture in 1941, and in 1945 joined the faculty of the Architectural Association School of Architecture in London. Korn captivated several generations of students "with his very un-English enthusiasm for the subject of architecture." His lectures in London drew large crowds, and sometimes ran late into the night.

Max Taut arranged for the architecture department of the Berlin Academy of Arts to have Korn named a special member. He accepted the honor "with great pleasure." After Arthur Korn retired in 1966, he moved to Austria, where he died in 1978.

———

Siegfried Weitzmann emigrated to Palestine in 1936. He was retrained there as a surveyor, and attempted to learn the Hebrew language, which he found exceedingly difficult, as did many German Jews. Already past the age of fifty, "he eked out a living by selling liquor," his second wife recalled, "going uphill and downhill in Jerusalem, despite his deteriorating heart condition." Eventually he managed to find work at a construction company, and wrote a book called *Study of Kafka*, which was published posthumously. Weitzmann's book contained descriptions of his own experiences as a victim of German tyranny, as an uprooted Jewish emigrant and survivor: "The judgment," he quoted from Kafka's *The Trial*, "does not come all at once; the proceedings gradually merge into the judgment." Weitzmann added this interpretation of Kafka's words: "There is absolutely

View from the fourth floor of the factory, 1931

no pronouncement of a sentence: the defendant learns neither whether he has been found guilty nor when the judgment will be executed—until it is actually executed upon him." In March 1960, Siegfried Weitzmann died in Tel Aviv.[28]

Nearly all the buildings Korn and Siegfried Weitzmann constructed between 1922 and 1934 have been destroyed. And the friendship between these two architectural masters came to an end in 1937 because of a woman.[29]

In August 1990, Edgar Fromm applied for restitution of the Fromms Act working capital, the factory premises in Köpenick, and the real estate in Friedrichshagen on his own behalf and that of the widows of his brothers Max and Herbert at the Office for the Settlement of Disputed Property Claims in Berlin. He retained Petra Benoit-Raukopf, a lawyer in West Berlin, to handle the legal work. Her background, in brief, was this: She was the daughter of the Czech communist writer Otto Katz, who survived the Nazi years in French, British, and American exile and published under the name André Simone. After the war, Katz returned to Czechoslovakia and worked as editor-in-chief of the party newspaper *Rude Pravo*. In 1952 he and ten Jewish codefendants were found guilty of "Zionism" during the Stalinist, anti-Semitic Slánský trial in Prague, and they were hanged. All the non-Jewish defendants received prison sentences. His ashes and those of the other executed men were mixed into the road grit used in the winter by the Prague sanitation department.

In the hope of expediting the return of the properties, Edgar Fromm traveled to Berlin in the summer of 1991 to meet with officials at the Treuhandanstalt (the post-reunification privatization agency for East German enterprises), which was about to sell the site in Köpenick. This agency was located in the former Air Force Ministry of Hermann Göring. The meeting left Edgar Fromm reeling. The official who spoke with him was cordial, but he explained that this was no easy matter. "Look here," he added by way of explanation, "I am working on the case of a gentleman in Israel who is ninety-three years old and in poor health. He will probably not live to see payment of the restitution."

Edgar Fromm, who died in 1999, lived to see his restitution payment validated. In July 1994, the Office for the Settlement of Disputed Property Claims confirmed the legitimacy of the heirs' claim to the property in Köpenick. But since the Stinnes Corporation had already invested money in it, a simple return of the property was deemed unfeasible, and the Treuhandanstalt had to pay out the proceeds of the sale to the heirs.[30] Edgar Fromm had died by the time reparations were finalized for the real estate in Friedrichshagen. In 2006—a full sixteen years after the application for restitution had been submitted—Petra Benoit-Raukopf was finally able to close the file for the restitution of the property, but the file on the restitution of the firm's working capital remains open nineteen years later.

FROMMS ACT FOR GÖRING'S GODMOTHER

JULIUS FROMM WAS FAR TOO PREOCCUPIED with his company to show much interest in politics. He usually voted for the Deutsche Volkspartei (German People's Party), whose business-friendly agenda meshed with his own interests. Besides, he quite liked the fact that the head of the Deutsche Volkspartei, Gustav Stresemann, was married to the daughter of a Jewish industrialist.

When Hitler became Reichskanzler in 1933, Fromm's two directors in the company were Berthold Viert and Karl Lewis. Viert had joined the National Socialist German Workers' (Nazi) Party quite early, on October 1, 1930 (his membership number was 336158), and later served as the acting head of the local chapter in the Berlin suburb of Hirschgarten. Lewis joined the Nazi Party in 1933.

It appears that Fromm approved of, and even welcomed, the political activity of his two managers, hoping against hope that it might protect his company from outside pressures. In any case, a red swastika flag and a picture of the Führer were soon displayed in one of the two cafeterias. In early January 1933 (during the final weeks of the Weimar Republic), Fromm suddenly started emphasizing the German nature of his merchandise, calling his products "pure German quality products." He soon began labeling his condoms "the bestselling German select brand." In an evident attempt to ward off boycotts of his Jewish company, he announced that "the sale of our Fromms Act select brand is, as always, absolutely permitted!" This announcement was printed on March 25, 1933, on the title page of the drugstore journal *Der Drogenhändler* in an old-fashioned German penmanship style known as Sütterlin script. In the next advertisement, Fromm left off the foreign word "Act" in the company name. For a brief period, he was so plagued by uncertainty that he refrained from advertising his condoms altogether, and focused on another of his products—Fromms Rubber Pacifiers—to show consumers that his products were in line with the Nazi campaign to step up the birth rate.[31]

"When my father was faced with the question of whether to leave Germany after the Nazi takeover," Edgar Fromm recalled, "his initial reaction was: 'Hitlers come and go. . . .'" Julius Fromm simply failed to grasp how deadly serious the National Socialists were about expelling and later annihilating the Jews. He insisted: "I cannot imagine this happening. After all, we are Germans!" Both of his directors, who had become Nazis, assured him repeatedly: "But Herr Fromm, we don't mean *you*. You're an exception."

Although the Reich Economics Ministry generally gave Fromm's company favorable treatment, since it made such a positive contribution to the German balance of trade, the company nonetheless became an ongoing target of harassment. As early as March and April 1933, an "in-depth" special audit of foreign currency regulations was conducted by the tax office. However, "no violations of any kind" could be detected. In addition, a "pure Aryan" competitor called Blausiegel, based in Erfurt, attempted to use the new anti-Semitic state doctrine to its own advantage. Fromm had made plans—later abandoned—to establish a branch in England, and these plans had been approved by the Reich Economics Ministry some time earlier. In 1934 Blausiegel protested this initiative, using a combination of vicious racism and a heavy emphasis on "German know-how": "Up to now, the German production of condoms and pacifiers has had little real competition in most European nations; it would be dealt a serious blow if alien elements succeeded in establishing businesses of the same kind abroad by taking advantage of German know-how."[32]

Julius Fromm was hoping not to have to emigrate, but he laid the groundwork just in case. The first step was to convert Fromms Act to a corporation in which he held 98 percent of the shares and his plant manager Alfred Hausding the remaining 2 percent. Fromm's role in the company he had founded was henceforth

Directors Berthold Viert (left) and Karl Lewis, ca. 1935

restricted to the status of consultant. He drew an annual payment of 200,000 Reichsmarks plus 300,000 Reichsmarks from the firm's net profits, and retained possession of the buildings and machines.

The next order of business was to bring his two younger sons to safety. (Max had already fled to Paris in April 1933.) He sent Herbert, the designated successor to his company, to London in 1934, where he marketed condoms imported from Berlin, and in the same year he enrolled Edgar in a Swiss boarding school.

———

On December 20, 1933, the chief administrative officer in Potsdam filed an application with the Berlin police commissioner to review Fromm's naturalization process, which had taken place back in 1920. The legal basis for this review was a law enacted on July 14, 1933, to the effect that citizenship awarded to "Eastern European Jews" between 1918 and 1933 would be revoked if the naturalization was deemed undesirable "with regard to racial and national principles." This routine procedure was applied to some 15,000 Jews who had been granted citizenship during the years of the Weimar Republic.

The official questionnaire on file referred to Fromm by his birth name, Israel. The Berlin police commissioner reviewed the records on December 13, 1933, and noted in the margin:

There is no reason to continue granting Fr. German citizenship. He has fared well in Germany, he went about his business [during the war] and earned a good livelihood while other Germans did their duty and put their lives on the line for their country. When Fr. applied for German citizenship, he did not do so for the love of all things German and the German Reich, but simply in order to facilitate his business operations and to steer clear of the discomforts he would have had to accept as a foreigner in Germany, particularly during the war. It cannot serve the interests of the German people for these kinds of people to continue enjoying German citizenship. . . . In view of the fact that Fr.'s petition for naturalization was rejected back in 1914 and he was thereby recognized as an international Jew, the law of July 14, 1933, should apply to him as well.

The overall assessment was less harsh: "He has not displayed behavior inimical to the welfare of the people and state in any civic, political, cultural, or economic context."

A senior civil servant ordered that "Fromm be given the opportunity to make a statement." Fromm responded immediately with a letter to the chief of police dated January 4, 1934, reaffirming his loyalty to the state:

I established my industrial company in Berlin, and I have built it up—in the beginning as its sole administrator and worker all in one—from the most modest beginnings to the importance it enjoys today. My German outlook and my German diligence have enabled me, conscientiously and honestly, to become one of the highest taxpayers in my residential district of Zehlendorf-Schlachtensee. . . . Without a hint of arrogance, I can state that the company is well-known far beyond the borders of Berlin for its technical and architectural excellence and its steadfast pursuit of optimal facilities to promote good hygiene and working conditions; foreign customers and experts have quite often told me that it has become a sightseeing destination for Germany— and even for the world. That is my German life's work!

He also pointed out that he had donated ten thousand Reichsmarks to the Winter Relief Fund, and that even back in the days of the Weimar Republic, he had advocated requiring community service in place of "unsatisfactory volunteerism."

Fromm appended to the document an endorsement by Dr. Paul Stuermer, an avowed right-wing conservative and member of the Alldeutscher Verband (Pan-German League). Stuermer emphasized "the great popularity Fromm enjoys in the workforce and among experts" as well as his loyalty to the state, and the host of economic and personal consequences Fromm's loss of German citizenship would entail: "In view of Fromm's emotional rootedness in his wholly German family, denaturalization would do untold mental and physical harm not only to him personally, but to the German public interest, which would suffer significant material damage."

On January 19 and 20, 1934, the District Factory Cells Division of the Berlin Nazi Party also sided categorically with Fromm "because of our interest in maintaining and creating new jobs." The Nazi officials at this location feared for the future of the factory and drafted a detailed report about Fromm's plan to set up a heavy-duty rubber factory producing tires with outstanding traction. The plant would employ two hundred workers on opening

Advertisement in Der deutsche Drogist, *1934 (text reads: Fromms— German quality products, manufactured by German workers)*

day. The report, dated January 19, 1934, states: "The company can be regarded as exemplary in both its technical and its social facilities. Director Fromm is the executive of the entire business. In the course of a single generation, he has brought this factory from very modest beginnings to its current prominence. Nearly all the machines and facilities in the plant were built to his own specifications, and most are patented. . . . Stripping this man of his citizenship poses the risk that slowly, but surely, this factory will lose its standing, and if F. sets up factories abroad, the market for German exports will be lost there."

The response by the Chamber of Industry and Commerce in Berlin was decidedly unreceptive to this argument. Motivated less by job concerns than by class envy of a successful Jewish businessman, and possibly by a prickle of anticipation about getting their hands on the booty themselves, the gentlemen disclosed their take on the issue "in strictest confidence": "We are having particular difficulty seeing why denaturalization of Herr Fromm would represent any serious danger to the continued success of his business, let alone that it would make the company go under."

Advertisement in Der deutsche Drogist, *1937 (text reads: Celebrating our anniversary—25 years of service to the health of our nation)*

In the end, the chief administrative officer in Potsdam ruled in favor of Fromm. He emphasized Fromm's "impeccably German way of thinking," and voted "to uphold naturalization in this specific instance." On April 21, 1934, the Prussian secretary of the interior decreed, in consultation with the Reich authorities, that "the plan to revoke Israel Fromm's citizenship is being dropped." Furthermore, it was found that strictly speaking, it was unlawful to force Fromm to resume using his first name Israel, and the Berlin police department initiated proceedings to rescind the "change in first name of the Jew Julius Fromm." However, the matter was still pending when he emigrated in 1939.[33]

——

Apparently undaunted by all these dealings, Fromm kept at his business. Evidence of his calculated optimism was a major new marketing campaign with an array of advertisements he and his staff (whom he referred to as his "propaganda department") designed for the pages of the *Drogisten-Zeitung* in 1933 and 1934. The sweeping curved lettering used in these ads proclaimed that this product was "Heat vulcanized / Storable for 3 years / Transparent." The company sought to appeal to the journal's rather conservative readers with slogans in old-fashioned German cursive script; these ran the gamut from jingles ("Fromms Rubber Products are the ones to get—because this brand's the best one yet") to lists of selling points ("Admired, Reliable, Popular!"). A 1934 advertisement declared with simple pride: "World-Famous Brand: Fromms Rubber Products."

In 1935 Fromm marketed his sheer condoms as "The Winning Quality Brand!" During the Olympic Games in 1936, he distributed a mass transit map to foreign guests with the "authorization of the Propaganda Committee for the Olympic Games." This map bore the title Nahverkehrsplan, a clever pun on the double meaning of the German word *Verkehr* ("transportation" and "sexual intercourse"), and thus a tie-in to his leading product.

Julius Fromm was busy around the clock, as a merchant, a boss, and an advertising agent on his own behalf. On top of that, he sought to advance the technology of his condoms. In view of the growing shortage of raw materials, Fromm—in collaboration with I.G. Farben in Leverkusen—conducted experiments to develop a suitable synthetic form of rubber.[34] He improved the lubrication of "rubber products for rectal and vaginal use," and filed a patent application to the Swiss Bureau for Intellectual Property in Bern on February 24, 1936. His new approach remedied several vexing problems that commonly occurred with older methods, which typically employed fine-grained materials such as Indian tragacanth or locust bean gum as lubricating substances. Although this treatment "smoothed the surface of the rubber products and improved the desired lubrication," the rubbers would swell up prematurely in humid air, causing an "annoying stickiness" and making it "very difficult to impossible" to unroll them. Fromm therefore mixed the bulking agents "with finely powdered additives unaffected by humidity, such as talcum, mica, and other substances of that sort" and dusted the rubber products with these mixtures. This patent may well have been his most important one. It was registered in thirty countries.[35]

———

In the summer of 1936, the anti-Semitic newspaper *Der Stürmer* launched a smear campaign. Under the headline "Yet Again the Jew Company Fromms," the paper used the form of ostensible or actual letters to the editor to inform its readers: "Dear *Stürmer*! I have before me edition no. 8 of the trade journal *Der deutsche Friseur* (The German Barber), dated April 16, 1936. On page 26 of this paper, I find a large advertisement for the Jewish company Fromms." Another letter writer described the conduct of

the *Gubener Zeitung* as "an outrage" and "the height of tasteless-
ness" for having placed an advertisement by "the Jewish company
Fromms Rubber Goods . . . right in the middle of the text of a
speech" by Rudolf Hess. Furthermore, the streetcars in Hamburg
were "still full of Fromms posters." "Couldn't you," the alleged
reader asked "dear *Stürmer*," "at least drop a broad hint to the
management of the Hamburg streetcars?"[36]

Julius Fromm was bound to have realized by this point "that
he had to leave Germany," his son Edgar recalled, "but he was so
successful that he did not want to give up." By the end of 1937,
he knew it was time to go. He instructed his bank, the Reichs-
Kredit-Gesellschaft, and his attorney, Sally Jaffa, to sell Fromms
Act.[37] The managers at the Reichs-Kredit-Gesellschaft agreed in
principle to lend Fromm their support. Their initial plan was to
grant him a credit in the amount of one million Reichsmarks so
that he could emigrate as quickly as possible, and to take interim

*The boss in his office in
Köpenick, ca. 1935*

possession of the company on behalf of the bank. The company could then be Aryanized in good time. But in May 1938, the legal situation changed drastically. From then on, sales of companies that belonged to Jews were subject to the approval of the Reich Economics Ministry.

Immediately thereafter, both the district economic adviser in Berlin, Professor Heinrich Hunke, and Hitler's economic adviser, Wilhelm Keppler, began to show an interest in Fromms Act. However, Hunke (who went on to head the economics division of the finance ministry of Lower Saxony after the war, and remained in that position until 1967) was pushed aside to accommodate a far more influential prospective buyer, and he instead took possession of the Ebro Company (officially called the First Berlin Steam-Horsehair Spinning Factory, Inc.) in Berlin-Weissensee.[38]

On May 18, 1938, a Dr. Heuser, the assistant district economic adviser, came to the Reichs-Kredit-Gesellschaft to discuss the

*One of the cafeterias in Köpenick, with a
picture of Hitler over a swastika, ca. 1935*

Fromm situation. According to notes on the conversation, he "pointed out that managing a factory with these notorious products would not be very pleasant for a bank, even if a trustee were appointed. Criticism of the bank might be leveled by a public authority or by some other agency." He added the ominous remark, "Lending a million to the Jew Fromm could be somewhat risky." After all, there was no guarantee that the collateral would ever be realized, even if it had been secured in line with standard bank procedures. From "the political standpoint," this business was "fraught with extraordinary risk."

Heuser threatened the bank, which was prepared to conduct reasonably fair negotiations with its client, Julius Fromm, that he would put a stop to the allocation of natural rubber to Fromms Act. After all, he pointed out, raw materials were subject to foreign exchange and armaments regulations. This action would have bankrupted the company and rendered the bank collateral worthless. And Hermann Göring—the man in charge of foreign currency and raw materials used for armaments—already had his eye on the ultramodern factory. As a result, Heuser explained, he himself would look around for a "financially solvent candidate for Fromms." The bank managers expressed their delight by underlining that part of the statement twice in their memo and adding three exclamation points in the margin.

The fact of the matter was that the prospective buyer had already been identified. This buyer and her associate were applying every conceivable kind of pressure to reduce the price of the business. Accordingly, the Reich Economics Ministry turned down a potential buyer whom Fromm had proposed. His name was Walter Koch, an Aryan German who lived in London. In the summer of 1938, Koch offered £50,000 for the business. The contract was even ready for signature.[39]

At the beginning of the sales negotiations in 1937, Fromm and the managers of the Reichs-Kredit-Gesellschaft had estimated a market value of five million Reichsmarks as a starting point, in view of the attractive Köpenick factory and the rising sales. In the course of the next six months, Fromm cut his initial asking price in half. Eventually the Reich Economics Ministry brought in a buyer named Elisabeth Epenstein, a woman who was offering to pay 200,000 Swiss francs to Julius Fromm from a bank in Zurich. According to the official German exchange rate, this sum was the equivalent of 116,000 Reichsmarks, but in reality the offer was worth several times that amount. After all, this was "precious western foreign currency," as people said at the time. The Reichsmark was regarded as play money abroad—just as the East German mark would be many years later—and was traded far below the official exchange rate.

Fromm was also granted the right to convert 300,000 Reichsmarks of his personal assets into £30,000 over a period of time, and to have unrestricted use of this money from abroad. That was a significant concession in those days and conferred substantial privileges on Fromm in comparison with other Jews forced to emigrate. The rest of the deal, which was approved by the Reich Economics Ministry, provided for Fromm to receive a share of 10 percent on Fromms Act export sales to British Empire countries. This share of the export sales would count as part of his personal assets toward the £30,000. He would then reimburse the now-Aryanized Fromms Act for the official equivalent value of his share of the export sales from his personal assets left behind in Berlin, which he—like all others hounded out of the country—would not be permitted to take with him. It appears likely that there had been an additional provision legally entitling Julius Fromm to sell all Fromms rubber products throughout the British Empire.[40] When the war broke out, this deal essentially became null and void.

The conditions of sale listed above for Fromms Act in July 1938 were dictated by a Dr. Siegert, an ambitious assessor in the Reich

Economics Ministry. He summoned Fromm to the ministry by telephone, refused to make any concessions, and "demanded notarization the very same day."

The compulsory contract was drawn up on July 21, 1938. On August 4, 1938, Dr. Carl vom Berg notarized the inequitable arrangement and had this to say in the preamble about the seller: "The person appearing before me is a Jew." A few days later, the Berlin chief of police approved the sale, and it was again declared with notarial authorization "that the company is to be regarded as an Aryan company from this day forward."[41] The new owner of the company was Baroness Elisabeth Epenstein von Mauternburg, who was advised by her lover, a Viennese businessman named Otto Metz-Randa. She was the godmother of Hermann Göring, who had arranged for her to get the factory because it worked to his personal advantage.

As wretched and demeaning as Julius Fromm must have found the outcome, his compulsory sale turned out reasonably well in comparison to other Aryanizations at that time. After all, a rela-

Julius and Selma Fromm in St. Moritz, 1937

tively substantial amount of foreign exchange was made available, albeit less than Koch would have paid. On September 30, 1938, the Reich Economics Ministry formally granted the transfer of 200,000 Swiss francs to the Schweizerische Kreditanstalt in Zurich, with the request "to expedite the matter." The document stated that "Herr Julius Fromm [is] free to dispose of the funds for the purpose of emigration."[42]

Officials at the Reich Economics Ministry made a note in the Fromms' passports permitting them to leave the German Reich at any time and without additional formalities. That note later proved problematic. According to Edgar Fromm's report, the British asked: "Why were you able to leave without any difficulty when many other Jews were not?"

Julius Fromm had lost a great deal, but not everything. He was set to start a new life in England. However, Germany went to war and put a crimp in his plans.

In 1946 the Fromm family's lawyer justifiably claimed: "The contract was signed under duress, and the payment was in striking disproportion to the value of the objects and shares acquired. Frau von Epenstein took advantage of her relationship with Göring, and at the Economics Ministry Herr Fromm was simply informed that the sale had to take place without delay under the set of conditions presented there."[43]

Just how much more valuable Fromms Act was in reality is evident from a capital adjustment completed in the spring of 1942 for tax purposes. Instead of 200,000 Reichsmarks of common stock capital, the internal revenue service set the value at one million. According to the balance sheet of December 31, 1940, the working assets came to 2,174,000 Reichsmarks. When the business was later bequeathed to the purchaser's lover, Otto Metz-Randa, the tax office set the inheritance tax at 939,000 Reichsmarks. The heir took this sum of money as a "credit" from the company's cash holdings without any liquidity problems.[44]

The business flourished during the war as well, and the work-force was supplemented by 150 foreign forced laborers in 1942.[45] Between 1942 and 1944, three barracks were built to accommo-date the new workers on the grounds of the Köpenick factory. The army needed finger cots for military hospitals and a supply of condoms in bulk. The regulations for army brothels in occupied France stipulated that each of the rooms had to display a sign that said "Sexual Intercourse Without Condom Protection Is Strictly Forbidden!" The sign had to be placed "in a highly visible loca-tion" and feature "letters that could be read easily from a distance of 20 feet." The women were required to make condoms avail-able, and the "price of the rubber prophylactics" had to appear on the inside of the door on the full list of set prices.[46]

Julius Fromm had always run his business with an iron fist, and had enforced a strict ban on smoking because of the fire hazards associated with the inflammable solvents used in the factory. To prevent employees from secretly enjoying a cigarette, matches and lighters had to be handed over when entering the factory premises. But within days of Fromm's departure from the company he had founded, the German employees demanded that the ban on smok-ing be lifted, a demand that the ever-cautious Fromm had consis-tently refused to give in to. "Our members," the new management wrote to the building inspection department in October 1938, "have repeatedly requested that one of the cafeteria rooms be reserved for smoking." The "pure Aryan" management immediately agreed to satisfy the demand for this wholesome indulgence in cigarettes, and confirmed that "there would be no danger in making a cafete-ria room available for smoking if the appropriate caution is exer-cised." This matter was pressing, it turned out, because "a social gathering" was coming up.[47]

A Critical Look at the Personal History of a Public Figure

SHORTLY BEFORE HERMANN GÖRING ESCAPED the hangman's noose in October 1946 by swallowing a potassium cyanide capsule, he fantasized, "In fifty or sixty years' time there will be statues of Hermann Göring all over Germany. Little statues maybe, but one in every German home."[48] A self-image this overinflated fits the impression of Göring as a robust, good-natured, and popular man. Unlike the ascetic and fanatic Hitler, or Joseph Goebbels, who was consumed by ambition, Göring had a crude barroom humor that people found appealing.

According to the British historian Richard Overy, Göring, the corrupt hedonist, embodied "the restless and violent nature of the National Socialist movement as a whole." He spurred on economic preparations for war and, in conjunction with this, the theft of Jewish property. In the authoritarian anarchy of the Third Reich, he moved through a total of twenty-eight top positions and titles, from Reich Hunting Master to Reich Marshal, from Reich Minister of Aviation to Prussian Prime Minister to Reichstag President to Commissioner for the Four Year Plan.

If there had been a title of Reich Lord of the Castle, it would have gone to Göring as well. No other leading National Socialist took more pleasure in amassing grand manors or reveling in historical kitsch, which explains his eagerness to get the successful and highly profitable Fromms Act into the hands of his godmother, Elisabeth Epenstein von Mauternburg, knowing that in return she would make him a gift of two medieval castles. To understand his interest in trading a condom factory for a citadel setting steeped in a sovereign past, it helps to have a look at the Göring family history.

In contrast to most prominent Nazi Party members, the second-in-command could trace a lineage of ancestors who were high-level Prussian civil servants. His forefathers included a military adviser to Frederick the Great and a district chief executive. His father, Heinrich Göring, who was born in Emmerich in 1839, earned a law degree, served as cavalry officer in the Prussian army in the wars of 1866 and 1870/71, and, after the foundation of the German Reich, became a district court judge. Heinrich Göring attracted

Postcard view of Neuhaus an der Pegnitz with Castle Veldenstein, ca. 1938

Bismarck's attention with an 1884 memorandum urging the development of a colonial policy, whereupon Bismarck sent him to London to have a look at the efficient way the British ruled and exploited their colonies, and thus acquire the basic knowledge that the Germans lacked. Göring was a widower with five children. While in London, he married for a second time. His new wife was Franziska Tiefenbrunn, a Bavarian peasant girl and beer garden waitress who was a good twenty years his junior. Shortly thereafter, he was sent as governor general to the "protectorate" of German South-West Africa (present-day Namibia).

Once in the protectorate (through which he was driven in the same travel coach that Bismarck had used during the war against France), he and his wife got to know and enjoy the company of Hermann Epenstein, a doctor from Berlin and a former medical officer in the Prussian army who owned quite a bit of real estate and pursued his passion for hunting in Africa. He became Frau Göring's doctor, and delivered her first son.

Castle Mauterndorf, 2006

Epenstein became a close friend and benefactor of the Görings. As the years went by, the childless bachelor became the god-father of the couple's three sons and two daughters. There is much significance in the fact that the Görings' second son, Hermann, who was born in 1893 in the Marienbad sanatorium near Rosenheim, was named after his godfather.

The elder Göring returned to Berlin after five years in Africa and six years as consul general and minister resident in Haiti. He and his family were now enjoying a lavish lifestyle in Berlin-Friedenau. The house belonged to their friend Epenstein. By this time, an intimate relationship had developed between Dr. Epenstein and Franziska Göring. This arrangement was quite beneficial for her family, which depended on her husband's rather modest civil service pension. Epenstein later allowed the Görings to live rent-free in one of his two castles.

Werner Maser's biography of Hermann Göring characterizes Epenstein as a "rich, cultivated, and artistically inclined Jew . . . whose penchant for luxury knew no bounds." Actually, it was Epenstein's father who had been Jewish, but he had converted to Christianity before marrying the daughter of a Catholic banker, and he had his son baptized as well.

In 1894 Epenstein purchased the rather dilapidated Mautern-dorf Castle in Lungau, Austria, on the southern slope of the Hohe Tauern mountains, and had it restored at great expense. As a re-sult, Emperor Franz Joseph I of Austria bestowed a title of nobility on the generous developer on August 8, 1910 and thenceforth he was known as Hermann Ritter Epenstein von Mauternburg. He had bought a second rundown castle in 1897 for twenty thou-sand gold marks: Castle Veldenstein, thirty miles northeast of Nuremberg. Sparing no expense, he commissioned a stonemason to restore it. This project took ten years to complete, and ran up a bill for the then-exorbitant sum of one million Reichsmarks.

Left to right: Hermann, Paula, Albert, and Olga Göring with their godfather Hermann Epenstein, ca. 1902

Once the renovations of Castle Veldenstein were complete in 1901, the Göring family moved in with Epenstein. According to the official Göring biography written in 1938, eight-year-old Hermann would have preferred to stay in Berlin at first, but he quickly changed his mind: "When he arrived in a horse-drawn carriage at the side of his father, and the road took them higher and higher, through the big castle gate and then through a second one, whose battlements and crenels struck him as even more beautiful; when he finally stood in the uppermost bailey, the castle tower, the deep well, and the vine-covered castle walls before him, the young Hermann's heart soared." "You really must come to Castle Veldenstein," Göring's sister Olga later told the friends of her now-famous brother. "This is where he spent his romantic youth, reading legends and dressing up as a knight, day in and day out. There you will be able to understand him."

Göring's father, who had become an alcoholic, spent his nights on the ground floor of the castle; his wife's bedroom was one floor

Left to right: Hermann Epenstein von Mauternburg, Hermann Göring, Elisabeth Epenstein von Mauternburg in Mauterndorf, 1916

above, adjacent to Epenstein's ornate chamber. The ménage à trois of the two Görings and their benefactor went on for fifteen years, until early in 1913, when Epenstein announced to Franziska that he had fallen deeply in love with another woman and would be marrying her soon. The woman's name was Elisabeth Schandrovich Edle von Kriegstreu. She was thirty-six years younger than the wealthy knight. Born in Temesvar, which was then part of Hungary (and is now in Romania), she was the daughter of a Prague aristocrat and a Bohemian officer, and had grown up in Budweis (today Budějovice in the Czech Republic) and Aussig (in the Sudetenland). Epenstein's niece recalled that "Aunt Lili" was "a radiant beauty." When she was seventeen, she had married and quickly divorced. Now, at the age of thirty-three, she met Ritter Epenstein von Mauternburg, who was fatherly and immensely wealthy. A few short weeks after the new lady of the manor moved in, the Görings were asked to vacate the castle grounds after having spent twelve pleasant years there. They moved to Munich. Heinrich Göring died a few months later, in December 1913.

The close relationship between Hermann Göring and his god-father, whom he regarded as a second father, remained intact. When Göring was severely wounded in 1916 as a fighter pilot, he stayed with the Epensteins at Mauterndorf Castle. At the end of his convalescence, he traveled to Castle Veldenstein with Elisabeth Epenstein, whom he called Lili, and who saw herself as the godmother of the Göring children and friend of their widowed mother. Göring's mother awaited them there. Göring later married Carin von Kantzow, a Swedish woman from a poor family with an aristocratic heritage. He also joined the National Socialist Party and had to flee the country in the aftermath of the failed Nazi putsch in 1923. Through it all, he continued his friendship with the Epensteins.

Immediately following the annexation of Austria in March 1938, he and his second wife, Emmy—Carin Göring had died in 1931—visited Mauterndorf Castle. He arrived with a large military escort and enjoyed an enthusiastic welcome. The lady of the manor was in a gloomy frame of mind, however. Her husband had died in 1934, at the age of eighty-four, and she was anxious about her godchild Albert (Göring's younger brother), who was working in film studios in Vienna and made no secret of his antipathy for the Nazis. She also feared that the National Socialists would start a war.

It is not known whether Göring and his godmother took this occasion to discuss the swap of Fromms Act for castles that took place shortly thereafter, but it seems likely. After the death of her husband, Elisabeth Epenstein had found a new partner, a retired Viennese lieutenant colonel and merchant named Otto Metz-Randa. "He was not handsome, but he was charming," Frau Epenstein's niece recalled, "and he knew something about finances." Metz-Randa saw little reason to own castles, since they just ate up money and yielded no profits. In his view, the more

On left: Hermann Göring in Mauterndorf, March 1938
On right: Aryanizer Elisabeth Epenstein, 1938

attractive option was to use the capital from Elisabeth Epenstein's historical real estate to make lucrative investments.

Whatever plan Göring and Frau Epenstein may have hatched
in March 1938, Göring was finally in a position to reciprocate
for the decades of his godfather's benevolence, and about four
months later, Elisabeth Epenstein bought Fromms Act. She
was also given a large piece of property—about 2,500 acres—in
Gösing (Lower Austria), which had a horse and chicken farm as
well as a luxury hotel with a staff of about a hundred workers and
administrators. It had belonged to the Jewish timber industrialist
Sigmund Glesinger of Vienna. Before he was able to emigrate to
the United States, he had to Aryanize his possessions. This trans-

action was surreptitiously overseen by Göring, and his godmother reaped the rewards. On December 16, 1938, Fritz Langthaler, the provisional manager, informed the district authorities: "The Aryanization of [Glesinger's] companies has been implemented with the authorized bill of sale, and I ask you to see to it that these companies are no longer listed in the directory of 'Jewish Businesses.' Heil Hitler."

The anti-Semitic novel *In the Shadow of the Ötscher* (1943), by an Austrian regional writer named Lorenz Peter Herzog, gives a fictional account of this case. Glesinger (called Schlesinger in the novel) is here the imperious "company president from Frankfurt . . . who buys up everything" and recklessly modernizes it: "Tear down the portal, remove bearing walls, a couple of crossbeams, concrete floor, done!" His plans are thwarted by "an alliance between Berlin and Vienna," which makes people like Glesinger "disappear at very short notice" and ensures that "an end is put to the bankers of the other race who are worth millions." In Gösing (called Hinterburg in the novel) "something was actually being done for the good of the community."[49]

———

February 1939 was the last time Elisabeth Epenstein visited the man who had helped her acquire the rubber factories and the country estate. He proudly showed her around Carinhall, his hunting lodge in Schorfheide, a vast forest north of Berlin. She then instructed her lawyer to transfer the ownership of Castle Veldenstein to Göring and his younger sister Edda as her gift to them.

Shortly thereafter she traveled to Chicago to visit her stepbrother. Before her departure, her lover, Otto Metz-Randa, persuaded her to draw up her will. The will named him executor of her estate. This document, which contained twenty-seven clauses, stated that Mauterndorf Castle was also to go to Hermann Göring.

Elisabeth Epenstein with her lover and adviser Otto Metz-Randa, 1937

Clause 14 read: "I bequeath my factory (Fromms Act Rubber Works), that is, the property and business as well as the property and business of the Fromms Act Rubber Works, Inc. in Danzig, to Colonel Otto Metz-Randa, Vienna V, Schönbrunnerstrasse 12." The country estate in Gösing also went to Metz-Randa.

He was not the only one slated to profit from the condom business. Elisabeth Epenstein directed that even if "the factories lacked the raw materials to continue operations, Frau Olga Rigele would be paid 1,000 Reichsmarks a month; Frau Göring, Berlin, 500 Reichsmarks a month; and Frau Paula Hueber 500 Reichsmarks a month" from the "rubber works" profits. These three beneficiaries were Göring's two married sisters and an unspecified "Frau Göring."

––––

During the war, Hermann Göring spent most of his time at the grandiose hunting lodge of Carinhall. He rarely visited Mauterndorf, but he did have a swimming pool built there. He lavished more attention on Castle Veldenstein, and in 1942 had an air-raid shelter constructed under the manor, with its own air, water, and electric supply. He also had the driveway paved with asphalt. On Easter 1945—with the Red Army already at the outskirts of Berlin—he paid a visit to Veldenstein in his *Schienenzeppelin* (a Zeppelin-shaped railcar). "Here he dressed down the contractors busy with the renovations," Eitel Lange, his personal photographer, later reported. "He said to the supervisor: 'I demand the fastest possible work from you and from every man in the contracting firm—now! If I return to find anything not in order, right down to the last nail, I will get nasty.'"[50]

No sooner had Elisabeth Epenstein returned to Mauterndorf from America on September 4, 1939, than she was found dead in her bed. Her niece, who still resides in Mauterndorf, attributes this sudden death at the age of fifty-three to her "chain smoking and constant coffee drinking to keep from getting fat."

Exile: Helpless in London

JULIUS FROMM WAS FIFTY-FIVE YEARS OLD when, in October 1938, he had to leave the country that had become his homeland. He and his wife traveled to Paris to visit their son Max, and a few weeks later they went on to London, where Herbert and his wife, Ellen (née Friedländer), were already living. Back in Berlin, Ellen's father had owned Friedländer & Grunwald, a company that made feather dusters; the factory was located in the same industrial complex on Elisabethstrasse where Fromm had for a time manufactured his condoms. Fromm had established excellent business contacts in the British Empire, which made London a logical choice for his forced relocation. He aimed to build on his past success and set up a new factory.

The British did not welcome the German Jews with open arms. For one thing, resentment of Jews ran deep in all social classes. "No doubt," Neville Chamberlain, Conservative Party prime minister, wrote to his sister Hilda in 1938, "Jews arent [sic] a lovable people."[51] For another, politicians were united in their belief that

Great Britain was not a country of immigration. The Conservatives aimed at achieving an ethnically and culturally homogeneous nation; Labour politicians and trade unionists did not wish to put their members in the position of having to compete with immigrants for the few available jobs.

The Aliens Act of 1905 had been put in place decades earlier to exercise greater control over the immigration of Eastern European Jews. Just a few days after the National Socialists came to power in Germany, officials noted a rapid increase in Jewish refugees. Since the visa requirement had been abolished for Germans and Austrians in 1927, the British border police had to stand by and watch as more and more newcomers masquerading as tourists or business travelers soon asked to be recognized as victims of religious and racial persecution so that they could apply for residence permits.

The officials in the Home Office Aliens Department quickly hit upon a pragmatic solution that would not cost the British taxpayers a single penny. The refugees would be permitted to extend their stay "provided that the Jewish community in Great Britain was prepared to guarantee, so far as might be necessary, adequate means of maintenance for the refugees concerned."

Apart from this, the British considered England a temporary stopping point for Jews, who needed to move on as soon as possible to the United States, or at least to a remote part of the extensive British Empire. However, Lord Bledisloe, the governor-general of New Zealand, was one of many who were concerned that "immigrants from Germany might be at heart, if not openly, Communists, and spread revolutionary propaganda to the social unsettlement of the local community." The Australian government chimed in with blatantly anti-Semitic arguments.

Julius Fromm entered the United Kingdom just as the political situation was coming to a head. After the Anschluss (annexation) of Austria and the ensuing smear campaigns against the Jews, thousands sought to escape to England, where the Jewish organizations were unable to meet the full financial needs of all the destitute refugees—many of them rendered destitute by the Germans. On May 2, 1938, the Home Office therefore reintroduced a visa requirement for Austrians; nineteen days later, this requirement was extended to Germans as well.

Julius and Selma Fromm had no difficulty obtaining visas. They could easily prove to the British Aliens Department that they were able to support themselves. At first the couple stayed at the Hotel Esplanade in London near Paddington Station. Sigmund Freud had also lived in this hotel, which was run by Austrian

Julius and Selma Fromm in their apartment
in London, ca. 1940

émigrés, after fleeing Vienna in June 1938. Later the Fromms rented a luxury apartment near Regent's Park.

No matter how comfortable their situation was, the Fromms were aware right from the time of their arrival in England that they were more tolerated than welcome. Like everyone else who had sought refuge in the British Isles, they were handed a card in German that read: "You are guests of Great Britain. Politeness and good behavior will ensure a kind reception and sympathy for you everywhere. Do not speak loudly in the streets, particularly at night. Be considerate about the comfort of other people, and avoid damaging the property and furniture of others. Never forget that England's opinion of German refugees depends upon your behavior."

The reverse side of this "welcome" card reminded them that "German refugees are urgently advised to exercise the utmost caution when speaking to others. For your own good, you are urgently advised not to accept any offers of employment without prior permission from the English government."

Julius Fromm tried to obtain permission to build a condom factory, but the plan went up in smoke when the war began, so he had to bide his time. The resulting forced idleness was very hard on this indefatigable man of action. In Berlin he had been in charge of more than five hundred employees and a worldwide sales network. Now he was reduced to ruling a small household with the same iron fist that had brought him success in Germany. Soup was set out on the table for lunch at precisely 12:30. Anyone who came late went away hungry.

———

Possessions tie you down. The more the German Jews had worked their way up and gained recognition, the harder it was for them to relinquish what they had earned and leave their homeland. Although Julius and Selma Fromm had fled Berlin, Julius's brothers and sisters hesitated to do the same.

Alexander had obtained a pro forma divorce from his non-Jewish wife and transferred ownership of the optician's shop to her. Even so, he was required to designate his big, beautifully equipped shop at Memhardstrasse 4, designed by Korn and Weitzmann, a Jewish place of business. The exterior had black marble and bronze panels with two curved cut-glass display windows leading to the entrance. Two film vending machines were installed outside. Glass sliding doors, built-in leather sofas, mirrored walls, and recessed ceiling lighting made for an inviting atmosphere for customers.

Alexander Fromm wrote up a report of the events surrounding Kristallnacht and the damage to his store: "As it was marked as a Jewish business in 1938, it was subject to the night of pogroms against Jews on November 9." All the store windows were broken, the inside décor—"optical instruments, all mirrors, glass cases, and cabinets"—destroyed, and "a large part of the goods" smashed or looted. In the later restitution proceeding, he esti-

Alexander Fromm, ca. 1950

mated that the "damage during the expulsion of the Jews on November 9" had amounted to twenty thousand Reichsmarks. "Right after Kristallnacht, the Gestapo came to the shop to take me into custody; I was saved only because I had already gone into hiding."[52]

Salomon Fromm's optician's shop was also ransacked and demolished on that infamous night. Siegmund, who, like Alexander, was married to an "Aryan," was taken away for a month to the Sachsenhausen concentration camp on the outskirts of Oranienburg, after which he was released, and required to report to the police on a daily basis for a full year.

By now, it must have been quite clear to Julius Fromm's brothers and sisters that they had to get out of Germany as quickly as possible. The now-Aryanized Fromms Act was interested in acquiring Fromms Cosmetics Associates, which belonged in equal parts to Siegmund, Bernhard, and Else's husband, Willy Brandenburg. On January 17, 1939, the three owners of Fromms Cosmetics had to appear before the notary Dr. Carl vom Berg on Bendlerstrasse, where Julius had been forced to sell his company. Fromms Act, owned by Göring's godmother Elisabeth Epenstein, and represented by Julius Fromm's longstanding directors, Berthold Viert and Karl Lewis, took over Fromms Cosmetics for a pittance: 16,700 Reichsmarks. The company's estimated market value was 100,000 Reichsmarks. The annual sales, as a former employee later attested, amounted to approximately 300,000 Reichsmarks, and the annual profit was 35,000 Reichsmarks.

The purchase price was to be paid out by the notary once the sellers had initiated the new owners into the production process. To this end, the three of them had to "make their workforce available to the buyer." The "sellers are obligated," the contract further stated, to dismiss without severance pay "the remaining two non-Aryan members at the earliest possible time." Since the cosmetics company was not deemed "strategically important for the war effort," it closed down in October 1942.

In early 1940—one year after the sale—the time for Siegmund Fromm and Willy Brandenburg to receive their money had finally arrived. (Because Bernhard had been expelled, he was deemed ineligible for any payment.) They were each given 5,075 Reichsmarks, but did not have unrestricted use of this money. The chief of police had issued an order for the purchase price to be reduced from 16,700 to 15,225 Reichsmarks, and the buyers were told to send an "equalization payment" of 1,035 Reichsmarks to the state treasury. Although the chief of police had dragged his feet on enforcing the payment of this reduced sum of money, he was much speedier when it came to enforcing punitive measures against the family. Since Bernhard, his wife, Lucie, and their son Frank did not have German citizenship, a

Alexander Fromm's shop in Berlin-Mitte, 1927

"prohibition on residence in the territory of the German Reich" was placed on the family a mere seven days after the compulsory sale, and their bank accounts were frozen.[53] Fortunately for Bernhard and his family, Julius Fromm, who had arrived in London three months earlier, could vouch for them, and their visas were expedited. They lost all their possessions, however. "We had to leave behind even our clothing and linens," Bernhard Fromm recalled after the war. "We could bring only a toothbrush and the clothes on our backs."

Soon Alexander and his family and Ruth also left for London. Friends had found Ruth a job as a domestic servant with a Jewish family. On April 19, 1939, she boarded an airplane in Berlin's Tempelhof airport. During the first week of September, her father, Sally, and his sister Helene flew out of Berlin. Julius had already financed Rudi Fromm's escape to South Africa as well. Rudi was the son of his brother Max, who had died in 1930.

Interior view of Alexander Fromm's shop, 1927

Julius rented a house at Canons Park in Stanmore, at the extreme northwestern end of London, for his relatives, but remarked in a rather businesslike manner a year later, "Unfortunately, I have provided a house for the whole family in order to keep the costs down. But because only Helene and Sally have moved in, it is now costing me a great deal of money."[54]

———

When World War II began, the already precarious situation of most Jewish refugees in Great Britain deteriorated still further. After the Wehrmacht invaded Poland on September 1, 1939, and both France and Great Britain declared war on the German Reich two days later, the British resorted to a security measure that had been widely implemented during World War I, the internment of enemy aliens. They were not alone in doing so. In France, all Germans were arrested indiscriminately; in the United Kingdom, however, it took several weeks for the Home, Foreign, and War Offices to agree on a course of action.

Soon 120 tribunals throughout the country were classifying enemy aliens from Germany and Austria (and then from Italy as well) into three groups. Class A was made up of people about whom there were serious doubts regarding their loyalty; they were interned immediately. Class C comprised refugees who did not arouse suspicions. Those who were neither overtly suspicious nor above suspicion were placed in Class B.[55] Their freedom of movement was restricted; for example, they were not allowed to go farther than five miles from their place of residence without police permission, and were barred from owning automobiles, cameras, binoculars, or weapons.

Nearly all of the 62,244 registered Germans and 11,989 Austrians, roughly 90 percent of them Jewish refugees, were summoned to the tribunals, which began their work in September 1939. Only 569 people were put into Class A, and 6,782 into B. The great majority, about 66,000, were classified as nonsuspicious and placed into Class C. Of those, 55,000 were granted the status of political refugees persecuted by the National Socialists.

Since the large majority of the tribunal staff members had no legal training, mistakes were bound to be made. Raimund Pretzel, who later became a renowned journalist under the name Sebastian Haffner, was assigned to Class A because he was not Jewish and thus could not prove that he had suffered persecution in Germany. In February 1940, he was interned in the county of Devon on the southern coast of England. There he met Jürgen Kuczynski, a Marxist historian, and Peter Jacobsohn, whose father, Siegfried, had founded the magazine *Die Weltbühne*. They had to spend the winter in unheated huts in a vacation complex patching up fishing nets.[56]

Most of the Fromm family members were deemed nonsuspicious and were placed in Class C, aside from Sally and his daughter Ruth. "The chairman of the tribunal," Ruth Fromm explained, "accused my father of having started out as an Englishman, then letting his citizenship lapse and eventually becoming German." He was therefore placed in Class B, and so was Ruth, in what amounted to guilt by familial association.

————

After German troops invaded Poland, they went on to occupy Denmark and Norway, and then overran Luxembourg, the Netherlands, Belgium, and France. The British faced a disaster in Dunkirk. Fortunately, 226,000 soldiers—nearly the entire British professional army—were able to escape across the English Channel to their homeland, but most of their equipment fell into the hands of the aggressors. Now the fear took hold of the otherwise stoic Britons that for the first time since 1066, invaders could occupy their island.

The fear of the "enemy from within," or of a "fifth column" of Nazi spies, assumed panic proportions. *The Daily Mail*, a mass-circulation conservative newspaper, ran a headline on April 20, 1940, declaring: "Act, Act, Act—Do It Now." The text read, in part, "All refugees from Austria, Germany, and Czechoslovakia, men or women alike, should be drafted without delay to a remote part of the country and kept under strict supervision." Other newspapers followed suit, and once Winston Churchill had succeeded Neville Chamberlain in the aftermath of Chamberlain's disastrous policy of appeasement, mass internments began—at first only along the English Channel and the North Sea, but soon throughout the country.

Early one morning, three policemen came to take Edgar Fromm from his parents' apartment. They brought him to barracks outside London. His cousin Ruth ended up in strict solitary confinement in the infamous Holloway Prison in North London. Only after six weeks and a hunger strike were she and her fellow sufferers allowed a few hours' daily recreation. Helene, Alex, and Bernhard Fromm were brought to an improvised camp; Herbert was deemed unable to withstand the rigors of detention and sent home to London after seven weeks. Fortunately for Julius, his wife, Selma, and Salomon, their doctor certified that at their age they could not be detained.

Edgar, who had just turned twenty and had recently fallen in love, was taken to Huyton, a transit camp near Liverpool.[57] Many of the internees were still teenagers; most were unmarried. Word soon got around that they would be sent overseas. Most volunteered to do so in hopes of escaping life in the camp. Edgar actually wanted to join the British army to fight against Nazi Germany, but the camp commander was adamant: "If you do not get on board of your own free will, we will force you to do so." Edgar later recalled, "They never let on *where* 'overseas' we would be heading."

After ten days in the transit camp, about eight hundred camp inmates, of whom about two hundred were German prisoners of war, were brought to the Port of Liverpool, where they boarded the troop transport ship HMT *Dunera*. The guards made it quite clear from the outset that this would be no pleasure cruise. With calls like "Move, you bastards!" and prods with rifle butts, they were herded onto the ship. The prisoners had to hand over their possessions, then submit to a body search. Whatever the guards considered worthless was thrown overboard. Edgar Fromm asked whether he could at least keep a picture of his fiancée. "In reply," he wrote in a 1957 report about his deportation, "a sergeant tore it out of my hand and pushed me down a spiral staircase."

No sooner had the *Dunera* pushed off to sea than a rumor that was as gruesome as it was true began to circulate. The first contingent of enemy aliens had sailed ten days earlier, at dawn on July 1, 1940, on the *Arandora Star*, a passenger steamer that had been turned into a troop transporter. After only twenty-seven hours at sea, the ship was hit by a torpedo fired by Günther Prien (who was later hailed as a submarine hero in Germany), and it sank off the west coast of Ireland. It took just a half hour for it to vanish in the waves of the Atlantic. Over six hundred Italians and Germans drowned, among them a former communist Reichstag representative, Karl Olbrich, who had fled to Great Britain by way of Czechoslovakia after spending three years in German prisons and concentration camps.

One of the 229 German survivors (most of whom were sent off a second time on the *Dunera*) was Peter Jacobsohn. Edgar Fromm was now on the *Dunera*, one of 2,646 prisoners cooped up behind barbed wire on a ship built for eight hundred passengers and bound for parts unknown. Two-thirds of the prisoners were Jews, but 200 Italian fascists and 250 German National Socialists and prisoners of war were also on board.

The internees slept in hammocks, on tables, in overcrowded cabins, or on the floor. There were no blankets. Soon a mixture of vomit and urine was dripping from the overflowing latrine

The Arandora Star, *sunk by a German submarine*

buckets onto the decks below. Food and drink were limited to tea and bread in the morning and afternoon, and there was cold soup for lunch. Two internees succumbed to disease en route, and another, overwhelmed with desperation, leaped overboard to his death. "At first we thought we were headed for Canada," Edgar Fromm recalled. "But when it kept getting hotter, and then we passed Sierra Leone, it dawned on us that they were bringing us to Australia."

Most of the guards on the *Dunera* were convicts released on parole. They looted the internees' luggage, and during a stopover in Cape Town, quite a few of them made off with their loot. Some were sadists who made the prisoners walk barefoot over broken glass. The officer in charge, Lieutenant Colonel William Scott, was unperturbed by this abuse, as documented in a message he telegraphed shortly before arrival to the Australian army department responsible for the prisoners of war. "The German Nazis," in his "personal view," had "exemplary" behavior, the message read. They are "of a fine type, honest and straightforward, and extremely well disciplined." By contrast, the Italians, Scott contended, "are filthy in their habits, without a vestige of discipline, and are cowards to a degree." The Austrian and German Jews, he declared, "can only be described as subversive liars, demanding and arrogant."

An impressive aspect of British democracy is that even in times of war it allows for criticism. Once the details of the "hell ship" voyage had come to light, journalists and politicians were heated about what was now being called the "*Dunera* affair," and about discrimination against Jewish refugees in general. The distinguished economist John Maynard Keynes spoke out on behalf of interned colleagues and declared that he had "not met a single soul, inside or outside government departments, who is not furious at what is going on." Victor Alexander Cazalet addressed the House of Commons on August 22, 1940, to condemn the "tragedies" on the *Dunera*, which he deemed both "unnecessary and undeserved": "No ordinary excuse, such as that there is a war on

The British troop transport ship Dunera

and that officials are overworked, is sufficient to explain what has happened," he fumed. One year after the *Dunera* affair, William Scott and several guards stood trial. Scott was court-martialed and his deputy sentenced to a year's detention.

After fifty-seven days at sea, the *Dunera* reached Sydney. Then Edgar Fromm and the majority of his fellow sufferers, about 2,600 in all, had to endure a nineteen-hour train ride before pulling into the town of Hay in New South Wales. Just outside the town, two internment camps—enclosed behind electric barbed-wire fences— had been set up so hastily that they seemed to have materialized out of thin air. Edgar was one of about a thousand Jewish deportees (some of whom had already spent time in German concentration camps) assigned to the spot in the desert designated as Camp 7.

During the day the temperature soared as high as 113 degrees Fahrenheit, and it was bitterly cold at night. Still, the food was good, and the Australians allowed the inmates to run the camp themselves. A former director of the Bavarian Mortgage and Exchange Bank helped them introduce their own currency. Doctors saw patients, an orchestra performed music, and young people completed their high school examinations. The prisoners put together a theater troupe and soccer teams. There was also kosher food for the Orthodox.[58]

Even before the British government publicly declared the indiscriminate internment and deportation a political blunder, the Home Office sent an envoy to the prisoners in Camp 7. This envoy was Major J. D. Layton, a Jew who in civilian life had worked as a London stockbroker. He offered the internees an alternative to remaining in Australia: anyone who volunteered to join the Pioneer Corps of the British Army could return to Europe.

Julius Fromm wrote to his son recommending that he stay in Australia and await the end of the war; at least he would be safe there. Edgar wanted to get back to England, however, come what may, so that he could marry his fiancée, Jolanthe Wolff. Jolanthe had been permitted entry into England in March 1939 because she had a household job lined up with the Fromms. Before long, Edgar and Jolanthe fell in love, but his father Julius was adamantly opposed to the match. For one thing, the woman Edgar had chosen was eight years older than he; for another, the factory owner considered a penniless servant not in keeping with their social standing—a strange sort of condescension, considering that Jolanthe's father had been a judge in Hamburg and her mother was a member of the Weill family, a distant relative of the composer Kurt Weill. Her forefathers had lived in Germany for a good eight centuries; the family's earliest known ancestors had emigrated from Spain in the thirteenth century, settling in Weil der Stadt near Stuttgart, from which they took their surname.

While Edgar was stranded in the Australian desert, he sent daily letters to Jolanthe. On December 23, 1941, after one and a half years overseas, Edgar Fromm came back to London and soon enlisted in the army. One year later, on New Year's Eve 1942, he and Jolanthe were married. His parents pointedly avoided the wedding.

Jolanthe Wolff's passport photograph, 1939

SEIZURE BY THE GERMAN STATE

IN 1938 GERMAN BUREAUCRATS began setting a complex and somewhat improvised—yet effective—machinery into motion. In a series of several dozen operations, they seized the assets the Jews had been forced to leave behind when they emigrated, placed them "in trust" for the German state, and eventually expropriated them. The loot was divided every which way. Although a substantial portion flowed into the Reich reserves for the benefit of the public at large, individuals eager to grab their share did not miss out. All across the board—from bigwigs and bourgeois to minions and manual laborers—there were profits to be had.

From London, Fromm gave instructions in 1939 to Günther Loebinger, an attorney and tax consultant in Berlin, to look after his remaining assets in Germany. Once the war began, Loebinger reported Fromm's various asset values to the Reich commissioner for the administration of enemy assets. Twelve dossiers were compiled to document every detail of Fromm's possessions. Copies of such important papers were always submitted to the Reich

Finance Ministry and directed to the attention of a senior civil servant named Ludwig Bänfer, thus laying the bureaucratic foundation for the expropriation to follow.[59]

Although Fromm had lost his German citizenship and was considered stateless in Great Britain, back home in Germany he was listed as an enemy alien, that is, as a Briton, once the British declared war on September 3, 1939. Compared to the legal status of a German Jew, this proved to be quite advantageous at first. The property he had left behind in the Reich was now subject to enemy asset administration, according to the standard principles of wartime international law. In the first year of the war, Loebinger continued to represent Fromm's interests using his power of attorney, but two resolutions by the Court of Appeal in Berlin, in November 1940 and in January 1941, resulted in the appointment of Werner Ranz, a lawyer and notary, as trustee; subsequently the attorney Karl Kühne assumed this function.

Günther Loebinger was born in 1899 in Schlesiengrube, outside of Beuthen (now Bytom in Poland), in Upper Silesia. Before he studied law in Breslau, he served as a volunteer in the German Army. He seems to have been an exceptionally judicious man, a real stickler for the rules. After 1939 he was forced to take Israel as his middle name, and because the job title "attorney" was now reserved for Aryans, his letterhead had to read: "Legal Consultant / Permitted to Advise and Represent Only Jews/ J.[ewish] ID: Berlin A 429165." His office was located in the Wilmersdorf district of Berlin, at Brandenburgische Strasse 38.

The Aryan business partners' behavior toward a man thus stigmatized was mixed. Some—including attorneys Ranz and Kühne—referred to him respectfully and without any discriminatory add-ons in their official correspondence as "Dr. Loebinger," acknowledging his legal degree. Others—mainly Julius Fromm's debtors—opted for the disdainful "Legal Consultant Israel Loebinger."

Owing to his service in World War I, Loebinger was not brought to the extermination camps when he was deported on July 1, 1943, but to Theresienstadt, on a transport for the elderly—the ninety-fourth *Alterstransport* from Berlin. Part of his furniture went to Albert Merten, a tax official from Teltow who had been bombed out shortly before that.[60] On October 28, 1944, Loebinger—together with 2,038 other prisoners—was transported from Theresienstadt to Auschwitz. Of them, 1,689 were sent straight to the gas chambers from the arrival ramp, among them the forty-six-year-old attorney Günther Loebinger.

———

On November 13, 1942, a group of undersecretaries of state decreed that expelled German Jews, who, like Julius Fromm, had actually or purportedly acquired citizenships in other countries were no longer to be treated as enemy aliens, but instead would be renaturalized as German citizens. The aim of this seemingly paradoxical measure was to subject emigrants to Reich laws, thus enabling the government to expropriate Jewish property still in Germany.[61]

For this reason, the Gestapo in Berlin now requested that the head of the security police and intelligence service conduct an "assessment according to [paragraph] 8 of the Eleventh Ordinance of the Reich Citizenship Law" in the matter of Fromm's property. The sole purpose of this ordinance, which was issued on November 25, 1941, was to take over the property of Jews holding German citizenship the instant they were deported. Paragraph 8 read: "(1) The head of the security police and intelligence service will determine whether the prerequisites for asset forfeiture have been met. (2) The administration and valuation of the assets is incumbent upon the Chief Finance Authority in Berlin." The latter had already set up the Asset Valuation Office in Berlin-Alt-Moabit for this express purpose. The Chief Finance Authority soon merged with the Chief Finance Authority of Brandenburg to gain the complement of civil servants required to carry out this massive theft from the German Jews.

Earlier, the Gestapo had called upon the Chief Finance Authority to secure Fromm's remaining assets from the Reich commissioner for the administration of enemy assets, but to hold off on their sale until a formal notice had been issued. The closing sentence of the Gestapo official Heinrich's letter ("I have closed my files") suggests that he knew exactly how the notice would read. The official notice of asset forfeiture followed on October 13, 1942. It was issued by Section IV B 4 of the Reich Security Main Office, headed by Adolf Eichmann, and signed by a man named Kube. Fromm's assets had been transferred from trustee administration into Reich property exactly one month before the undersecretaries of state got around to weighing in on this matter at their conference on November 13.

The Chief Finance Authority was delighted to announce that the involvement of trustees Ranz and Kühne was now a thing of the past. Kühne begged to differ. On January 13, 1943, he stated matter-of-factly: "The administration of enemy assets will not be terminated until a conclusion is pronounced by a ruling of the Court of Appeal." He refused to hand over the assets or settle his accounts until this ruling was made. Two days later, the pertinent application was filed by the Reich commissioner for the administration of enemy assets.

On March 9, 1943, Kühne was relieved of his duties by the Court of Appeal. This step by the judges of the Fifteenth Civil Court—Günther, Andrée, and Schroeter—put the finishing legal touches on Julius Fromm's expropriation. They declared that the entire fortune in Germany that had belonged to the London businessman Julius Israel Fromm was now "forfeited to the Reich." This fortune comprised a wide variety of assets.

———

On April 17, 1940, the Dresdner Bank had reported to the central tax office in Berlin that its client, Julius Fromm, had a credit balance of 294,267 Reichsmarks. There were also accounts at the Commerzbank and Privat-Bank with a balance of 21,134 Reichsmarks, as well as a balance of 12,814.97 Reichsmarks at the Deutsche Bank (as of December 31, 1940). An additional account at the Reichs-Kredit-Gesellschaft contained 14,917 Reichsmarks.

The Berlin tax office in Moabit-West issued a warrant of distress in the amount of 110,614.82 Reichsmarks "as a precautionary measure" for a portion of the account at the Dresdner Bank on June 8, 1940, as a first step in gaining control over the full sum of the assets. With the accrued interest, Fromm's bank balance had risen to 305,266 Reichsmarks by December 31, 1940, but a year later it was down to 112,639.65 Reichsmarks.

The Reich Finance Ministry on Wilhelmplatz

So what happened to the non-impounded shortfall of about 200,000 Reichsmarks? In 1941 the Finance Ministry used this money for the German war chest and turned it into Reich treasury notes bearing 3.5 percent interest.

By 1941 a substantial portion of Julius Fromm's savings had been transformed into a war loan, and his assets were being handled by the Reich commissioner for the administration of enemy assets. Historians still tend to accept uncritically the view that this office generally "took prudent care" of the foreign property belonging to Jews, but this notion is patently false.[62] Even a cursory glance at the files reveals that these civil servants, who were allegedly so eager to stick to the letter of the law, made a point of stamping "Jew" on selected asset reports.

After the Court of Appeal had released Fromm's assets for transfer to the state in early 1943, the Chief Finance Authority submitted a printed form to the safe deposit section of the Dresdner Bank on June 7, 1943, ordering it to send "German Reich treasury notes V. 41 III 16J/D yielding 3½% interest in the amount of 195,500 Reichsmarks belonging to the Jew Julius Israel Fromm" to "the Deutsche Reichsbank, securities division." The Reichsbank was given a copy. But the key document was a printed form prepared especially for this sort of transfer: "To Patzer's Division of the Reich Finance Ministry."

Max Patzer was responsible for securities collected from Jews for the benefit of the Reich. He eagerly sought out ways to delete debt certificates from the German Reich debt register by using the mass expropriations from Jews to alter the national budget, creating new borrowings in their place without increasing the overall debt. The officials entrusted with this task were to leave no traces of these maneuvers. They were expected to obliterate each item "without recording the name of the individual Jew who had given the securities in payment."[63] The smoke screen did not work perfectly, however. In 1963 a document from the Reichsbank surfaced in the Berlin restitution office with details showing that Reich treasury notes issued to the name of Julius Fromm (including accrued interest) had been "realized on September 11, 1944, in the amount of 202,268.20 Reichsmarks" and were therefore no longer listed as war debts of the German Reich.

———

On a questionnaire about its client Fromm, the Berlin private bank Reichs-Kredit-Gesellschaft A.G. reported to the local central finance office on May 15, 1940, under the heading "Interest-bearing and non-interest-bearing receivables of every description": "It[em] 1 package (sealed) with the address: Israel Julius Fromm, Hotel Esplanade, 2 Warrington Crescent, London W 9, sealed and appraised by the sworn assessor." About a year later, the bank noted somewhat cryptically: "Safe deposit box settled. Holdings as of December 31, 1940, no longer available."

The bank had indeed delivered the mysterious package, in accordance with a decree by the Reich Economics Ministry dated July 8, 1940, to the Municipal Pawnshop, Dept. III, Central Office, Berlin, Danziger Strasse 64. There the unknown contents were treated like an unredeemed pawn item—they were sold. The Reichs-Kredit-Gesellschaft had requested that the equivalent value of the package be remitted to the emigrant account it held in Fromm's name. Although the law required this transaction, it did not take place, and the trail of the sealed package was lost. A tax office inspection stamp dated January 1944, bearing the text "2nd registration not applicable" on the 1940 registration form documents the fact that the money was pocketed by the German Reich.[64]

As the restitution proceedings later established, the package contained gold coins of various origins worth at least twenty thousand gold marks. It was also filled with Selma Fromm's jewelry, which included a pair of platinum earrings with two white diamonds; a pearl necklace with diamond clasp; a platinum necklace "made up of alternating diamonds and emeralds," a total of thirty gemstones, also with a diamond clasp; "a gold bracelet that was set with about ten rubies and ten diamonds"; and matching brooches, rings, and pendant earrings. The safe deposit box also contained gold wristwatches, cigarette cases in platinum or gold, a large gold men's signet ring, and other high-quality accessories.

After the war, the restitution office offered to pay 350 German marks for the lot. However, the District Court of Berlin set the value of the package at 202,320 German marks.[65]

————

"Client also has a steel box," the Deutsche Bank reported to the Berlin central tax office at Jüdenstrasse 59 on January 30, 1941, nearly a year after the safe deposit box had been turned over. No response. Displaying its own peculiar brand of dogged allegiance to the regime, the bank tried for a second time to notify the Chief Finance Authority of Berlin-Brandenburg on March 30, 1942: "The client also has a steel box." Just under a year later, the authorities instructed Eulert, the valuation officer, to remove the contents.

Because the keys for the box could not be located, the Deutsche Bank made arrangements for the Bode-Panzer Safe Factory, Inc., a locksmith company in Berlin, to "force open the box on Thursday, February 4, 1943, at 10 a.m." The costs of breaking and entering Fromm's steel box, and for the "repair of the box, making new keys, etc.," came to forty Reichsmarks. The Deutsche Bank simply withdrew this sum of money from the account of its long-standing customer.

Eulert made the necessary arrangements for opening the box. Recognizing that this procedure might invite corruption, he brought his colleague Otto Gottschalk along as a witness. The

*Interior view
of the Fromms Act
administration building
in Köpenick, ca. 1935*

branch manager Wilhelm Beutjer and the bank official Wilhelm Neumann appeared on behalf of the Deutsche Bank. Beutjer and Neumann prepared a report detailing the opening of the box, which included the following text:

> The Jew Julius Israel Fromm, who has emigrated to England, and who last resided in Berlin-Nikolassee, at Rolandstr. 4, rented steel box no. 57 at the N3 branch office of the Deutsche Bank in Berlin-Köpenick, according to a contract dated June 30, 1931. The assets of this Jew have been forfeited to the Reich in accordance with the Eleventh Ordinance of the Reich Citizenship Law of November 25, 1941. On orders from the Chief Finance Authority of Berlin-Brandenburg, the steel box of Julius Israel Fromm is to be forced open. The keys to the box could not be produced. The following witnesses in the N3 branch office are present . . .

This is how legally regulated plundering was carried out in the vaults of a German bank. The betrayal of a client and the breach of trust it entailed meant nothing to the bankers who were active parties to it. Eulert and the three witnesses affixed their signatures in perfect penmanship under the minutes of the meeting. The final paragraph closed with this sober comment: "After steel box no. 57 was opened by an employee of Bode-Panzer, Inc., in the presence of the three witnesses, the strongbox was taken out and jointly opened by the three witnesses." Beutjer, Neumann, and Gottschalk bent expectantly and patriotically over the strongbox. A handwritten note by witness Gottschalk included at the end of the official record stated what they discovered in this box: "nothing."

A few days later, Karl Kühne, the notary who was still the official enemy asset administrator at the time, was explaining the legal situation. As always, he skipped right past the "Heil Hitler" greeting and got straight to the point: "In any case, the steel box was opened without anyone consulting me." Herr Assessor Kühn of the Chief Finance Authority office informed him that "all this happened inadvertently" and he should contact the person responsible, an attorney named Gärtner in the Asset Valuation Office who was performing wartime public service duty. A written complaint was addressed to Gärtner, who scribbled a nasty "Why?" on the letter and left it unanswered.

———

Like every successful businessman, Julius Fromm had debtors. His outstanding accounts were also to be deposited to an account containing "assets forfeited to the Reich," administered by the Deutsche Reichsbank and listed as account number 1/1111. As a rule, the debtors were former business partners of Fromms Act whom the boss had helped out of financial jams with his own money, especially during the world economic crisis that began in 1929. He accepted real estate property as collateral for these debts, and the debts were duly registered in a land registry.

These transactions had to be reported to the Enemy Assets Administration in 1940. The reaction of the executives at the

Daubitz Rubber Company in Berlin-Rudow was typical of borrowers. Only after an official inquiry did they acknowledge having received from Julius Fromm, who was "reportedly in London," a loan in the amount of thirty thousand Reichsmarks—with no set maturity date.

Fromm's former business partners falsely claimed that they had been given the money without the expectation of paying it back as long as they themselves refrained from manufacturing condoms. Eventually they had to repay to the German Reich in full the loan that Fromm had extended to them against supply contracts.

The case of Otto Schultz, a pharmacist, affords unique insights into this matter. He ran a wholesale business at Chausseestrasse 87/88 in Berlin-Wedding, specializing in chemical photography equipment and Fromms Act products. Back in 1931, Schultz had borrowed ten thousand Reichsmarks from Fromm at an interest rate of 4 percent and used his vacation property in Zingst on the Baltic Sea as collateral. Three years later, Fromm waived any further interest payments.

When Schultz had to make a declaration to the Chief Finance Authority on April 12, 1940, he claimed that a large part of the debt had already been paid off. Some time later he demanded that at least part of the mortgage payable to Fromm be cleared. The debtor was hoping that by now, Fromm's official status had shifted to "evacuated Jew Julius Israel Fromm." But the Chief Finance Authority insisted on seeing proof of the alleged repayments. Schultz responded with a letter containing "explanations in lieu of sworn statements." He contended that in September and October 1938, Fromm had released him from repaying seven thousand Reichsmarks, but shortly thereafter "left for parts unknown," and as a result there was no written agreement.

The Chief Finance Authority insisted that the pertinent documents be produced, at which point Schultz suddenly recalled that

Bookkeepers at Fromms Act in Köpenick, ca. 1935

"the Jew Fromm" was in London. He had corresponded with him several times regarding this matter. On August 29, 1939, everything had been settled, but then—regrettably!—war broke out two days later. In late 1940, the management of the Reich postal service in Stettin expressed interest in the lovely Baltic Sea property on the Darss peninsula and wanted to use the building as a vacation center for its workers. Schultz was inclined to sell it, but in order to do so, he had to put the issue of the "Jewish mortgage" to rest once and for all on an official level. To prove that he had been released from this debt, he produced a friend named Erich Wallenhauer, who lived in Berlin-Steglitz. Wallenhauer was prepared to testify under oath that he was quoting from memory an allegedly "misplaced letter" sent by Fromm that confirmed Schultz's version.

According to an internal memorandum in early 1943, the head of the Asset Valuation Office was inclined to let the matter rest and accept a payment of 3,500 Reichsmarks. However, someone in the hierarchy decided to consult Schultz's local tax office and described the case to his colleague. The answer came by return mail: "Over the years, Schultz has declared impossible profits or losses, although his sales were consistently good. He has regularly submitted requests for deferral or exemption from payment. His bookkeeping does not add up. . . . In matters of taxation, I must deem him unreliable."

Schultz deposited 3,500 Reichsmarks into the account of the Chief Finance Authority at the Deutsche Reichsbank and again asked that the mortgage be canceled. However, the Chief Finance Authority was unyielding, demanding categorically on March 5, and then again on April 1, 1943, that the entire debt be paid—with interest. Schultz reacted on June 19 by applying for a deferral, since he was anxious to "produce new evidence." At this point he came up with a new addition to his string of lies, claiming that Fromm had not waived the debt of seven thousand Reichsmarks in 1939—as he had already testified twice under oath—but only of five thousand. And sure enough, nine days later the determined debtor located a "witness," an attorney and notary named Ernst Ziehe, who confirmed "as requested" and "with a Heil Hitler salutation" that he had in his possession a letter to this effect from creditor Fromm, dated August 16, 1939. He claimed to recall the matter quite well. The Chief Finance Authority was no longer interested, and on September 2 filed a complaint at the district court in Berlin. On September 17, Schultz paid "the Jewish mortgage" to the German Reich, and on October 6, 1943, the court cleared the mortgage in the land registry.

The administrators at the Asset Valuation Office had known the true situation for quite some time, because in February 1943 they had contacted the management of the Fromms company, where a copy of the letter that Julius Fromm had written to his old business friend from London (not in August, but in April 1939) was located right away. Fromm's tone was polite and accommodating, and suggested that Schultz pay him six thousand Reichsmarks in two installments, and Fromm would be happy to waive the rest. But Otto Schultz had ignored the offer. "No cash payment can have taken place," Fromms Act stated, since the expatriate "had emigrated in late 1938."

Julius Fromm dealt with his other debtors similarly, following the principle of "live and let live." But Otto Schultz, who had been working with Fromms Act since 1914, had the audacity to claim: "Unhappily, this Jew debt has been disastrous for me." In actual fact, he had used the money interest-free for nearly ten years.

"Jew Auction" as Aryan Haunt

FROM HAD PURCHASED THE PROPERTY at Rolandstrasse 4 for 95,000 Reichsmarks in 1919, then had it lavishly renovated and furnished. In 1933 the German Credit Bureau assessed its value "at 300,000 to 400,000 Reichsmarks."[66] When Fromm and his wife left Germany in October 1938, he did not sell the house, but instead arranged for Elvira Fromm (the wife of his brother Salomon), his sister Else, and her husband, Willy Brandenburg, to reside there.

Shortly before emigrating, Fromm also granted an official lifetime right of residence to Anna Frieda Scheffler, who had been the family's housekeeper for many years. When Frau Scheffler died on February 19, 1943, Karl Kühne, who was still the asset administrator, promptly reported her death to Herr Kühn, the assessor at the office of the Chief Finance Authority. By return mail, Kühn appealed to the district court to revoke the right of residence and at the same time to "transfer the entire property to the German Reich, represented by the Berlin-Brandenburg Chief Finance Authority, Berlin."

However, the Chief Finance Authority had already "entered into sales negotiations" at the end of 1942—ignoring Frau Scheffler's legally binding right of residence and the Jewish tenants, and disregarding the fact that the property was still being held in trust as an enemy asset. On November 20, 1942, the Asset Valuation Office accepted an offer from the Berlin-Charlottenburg city councilman Karl Sommer. On December 20, the property was assessed, and on January 18, 1943, it was inspected "to determine its adaptability for Reich purposes."

On February 13, the Chief Finance Authority notified the Reich finance minister that the house was well suited "to provide housing for civil servants," and that Sommer had offered the full asking price of 46,000 Reichsmarks "by telephone." Compared with the actual market value of the villa, it was a pittance. The chief councilman, Willy Bötcher, was handling this matter at the Asset Valuation Office. Bötcher and his boss, a senior government official named Hans Thulcke, indicated that party comrade Sommer was their first choice, and Sommer was eager to finalize the purchase. There were two compelling factors in his favor. For one thing, he had suffered an injury while serving the Third Reich— an unspecified injury that impaired 50 percent of the functioning of one of his limbs or other body part—and for another, the "report on his political activities," which he was happy to enclose with his application, gave him a glowing recommendation.

The deal fell apart when the Reich finance minister registered his fundamental objections to it. "I ask that the sale of the property be refused," instructed Walter Maedel, who was in charge of the Asset Valuation Office, and referred to a memorandum he had just issued on February 16, 1943.[67] About a year earlier, the minister had imposed a block on sales of nationalized properties from Jews, as Thulcke was well aware. That is precisely why he had focused on the loophole offered in "paragraph 3a, clause 1 of the decree of April 22, 1942—O 5300—443 IV," which permitted exceptions to be made for prospective buyers if they were disabled or had distinguished political service.

This case, and many others like it, made the Reich finance minister realize that he had to draw attention to the purpose of the restrictive regulation issued in April 1942, and to tighten it up.[68] Although both decrees ostensibly ensured that frontline soldiers could not be placed at a disadvantage as purchasers of formerly Jewish real estate, the Reich finance minister had a different motive for forbidding the sales: he wanted to force financially solid Germans to invest their money in life insurance or savings accounts, thus blocking any diversion into tangible assets. This was a deviously clever way to reinvest money entrusted to the banks or life insurance companies as war loans. In this way, the money flowed into the war chest "silently" (to use the financial parlance of the day). In addition, the Reich collected rent from the houses of those who had fled or been deported.

The former Fromm villa,
Rolandstrasse 4, 2006

On March 15, 1943, District Court Judge Heinrich Feussner certified in the land registry division of the district court of Berlin-
Lichterfelde that the property formerly listed in the name of
Julius Fromm had been transferred to the German Reich. The
section of the land registry marked "owner" now contained the
following information: "German Reich, represented by the Berlin-
Brandenburg Chief Finance Authority, Berlin." The court officials
explained the basis for this entry as follows: "By virtue of expira-
tion, in accordance with paragraph 3 of the 11th Ordinance of the
Reich Civil Code dated November 25 and entered on March 15,
1943."[69] The process was not regarded as a transfer in the legal
sense, but rather as an emendation of inaccurate wording. Paragraph 9.1 of the Eleventh Ordinance provided a justification for
this practice: "When entries in land registries expire and are thus
rendered inaccurate, they are to be rectified free of charge at the
request of the Chief Finance Authority of Berlin."

Once the sale of the villa to the Nazi official Sommer had fallen
through, the Chief Finance Authority looked to Colonel Wolf
Hagemann as a possible tenant, at the request of the urban planning office in Berlin. Hagemann, a professional soldier, was living in Berlin-Mitte, at Königstrasse 41. In 1919 he had served in
the volunteer corps in Silesia. He was awarded the Knight's Cross
of the Iron Cross in 1940 as a lieutenant colonel in the mountain
infantry at Narvik, and in 1944 the further distinction of Oak Leaves
was added to his Knight's Cross. To give this hero an attractive
residence, the Chief Finance Authority approved disbursement of
5,500 Reichsmarks for "work on renovations and additions" to
the Fromm villa despite the wartime building embargo then in
effect. Throughout the summer, the property was redesigned
under the management of Reich Building Bureau II. Hagemann
had an air-raid shelter built, and put in an additional bathroom,

an extra kitchen on the upper floor, and other luxuries. Hans Lüders, a senior official at the Asset Valuation Office, had to transfer a total of 8,500 Reichsmarks "from the expatriate's liquid assets" to cover these expenses. The building inspection department of the Berlin-Zehlendorf district office duly approved the renovations for Colonel Hagemann—on August 14, 1945.[70]

Before the Chief Finance Authority could begin upgrading the Fromm villa to conform to the wishes of the bearer of the Knight's Cross, a construction permit had to be secured, and the bureaucrats in this office had to be persuaded to expedite this predatory process. The Chief Finance Authority pressured Bailiff Curt Brückenstein to assess the inventory left behind after the deportation with notes marked "Special Assignment!" and "Extremely Urgent!" By this point, Gärtner had already called upon his colleague, Herr Korge, the civil servant in charge of furniture appraisal, to arrange for the sale of Julius Fromm's furniture on January 13, 1943.

Wolf Hagemann, awarded the
Knight's Cross, ca. 1940

The Evaluation Office disposed of the basic furnishings for a two-person household on March 20, 1943, for the price of 2,473 Reichsmarks. The purchaser was Colonel Max Bork, a member of the Wehrmacht general staff residing at Pfalzburger Strasse 15/1. Shortly thereafter he was promoted to general. Bork's wife, Else, selected the furniture and other items, which included two beds with night tables, a vanity, various freestanding closets, a leather sofa, a leather easy chair, dishes, a cabinet with glasses, fifteen coffee cups, and so on.

"The remaining items," Kühn, the assessor in charge of this matter, noted, "were brought to Korge and auctioned off there on May 17, 1943." We can infer from this note that the Chief Finance Authority had taken charge of the auction, instead of following the standard protocol of working with a private auction house. The auction at Korge's had been announced on the previous day in an advertisement in both the *Völkischer Beobachter* and the *Berliner Lokalanzeiger*. The advertisement made special mention of "1 lge. corner sofa with 12 wooden easy chairs (leather)." The seating was from Julius Fromm's household. The advertisement also enticed buyers of all social classes with "oil paintings, books, light fixtures, glass, fine china, household items, and many other pieces" for this "public" auction. It began at 9:15 a.m., and the items for sale could be inspected one hour beforehand: "Entrance only with photo identification and as long as seating is available. The Chief Finance Authority of Berlin-Brandenburg, Asset Valuation Office."

A man named Liebert, who lived at Chausseestrasse 59, purchased the elaborate corner seating unit for nine hundred Reichsmarks. Two pictures and a wall plate went to the family of Gustav Adolf Bächle at Prinzregentenstrasse 4 in Wilmersdorf. There must have been a good number of bids on the grandfather clock, because its price doubled. In the end it went to Otto Sander, a merchant who lived at Adalbertstrasse 14 in Kreuzberg, for the price of two hundred Reichsmarks. Small pieces of furniture and box springs proved to be hard sells, and went to a bidder named Gartz at Werder 96 for a price far below the appraised value. The family of Richard Piebus, an elevator operator who lived at Kottbuser Ufer, bought just a single round table. Friedrich Schilling, a painter residing at Motzstrasse 17, was out for antique liqueur glasses; he dealt in paintings and antiques. The sewing machine was auctioned to the Hofschulzes from Lüderitz (in the subdivision of Greater Poland the Germans referred to as Warthegau). Four lamps, a chair, and crystal and vases were acquired by Max Fischer, from the same town.

After a fierce bidding war, Franz Knabe carried off a round table, a sofa, a desk chair, and a batch of framed family pictures. The pictures were especially important to him. Knabe had a picture framing and molding business at Oranienstrasse 36 in Kreuzberg. Most likely he threw away the photographs of the Fromm family, polished the frames, and placed them in his showcase for purchase by newlyweds, young widows, and others who were delighted to discover that such nice things still existed.

A bargain-hunter named Hagen from Reichshof (Rzeszów) in occupied Poland bought glasses and a silver-rimmed carafe. Fine china went to the Schumann family at Kottbusser Strasse 6. Paul Gallisch, a postman who lived at Artilleriestrasse 13, paid a hundred Reichsmarks for Julius Fromm's marble desk set and a few small items. Two cardboard boxes and a basket filled with an assortment of household goods went to F. Marschall on Wassmannstrasse for ten marks. Borokowski, residing on Kirchstrasse, paid fifteen marks for similar items, as did M. Worieki of Lausitzer Strasse 21. The bidders whose identities could not be established in the 1943 Berlin address book (most of whom were evidently women) must have been lodgers, and thus of a lower social status.

The auction of the remainder of the Fromm household on May 17 yielded 2,255 Reichsmarks gross. The purchasers paid cash and hurried off with their loot. The end of the auction log contains the following comment: "The signatures of the highest bidders could not be obtained because they were no longer present at the end of the auction." The diary of Victor Klemperer gives us some indication of how the day must have "gone wild" in Klemperer's description of the "auction of the Jacoby possessions" in Dresden on December 7 and 9, 1942, in the "Jew house" in which Klemperer was living: "We have to keep our rooms locked because the place is crowded with people inspecting the goods. On the first day the auction was held in the hall—I looked on (from the gallery), never having seen one. Involved were small household effects, and the bidders were *menu peuple* [common people]. After that more expensive objects and a somewhat better-off crowd." On September 7, 1942, Jenny Jacoby, the octogenarian widow whose possessions would be sold off three months later, had been forced to leave her villa "with a cane, bent, but intellectually alert," and was sent to Theresienstadt.[71]

———

To return to the auction of Fromm's goods: the moving company Adolf Göritz issued a bill in the amount of 207.20 Reichsmarks for transporting the items from the villa in Berlin-Schlachtensee to the auction site at Kottbusser Ufer 39/40 in the Kreuzberg section of Berlin. The antiques dealer Georg Hinsche confirmed in an official statement that there were no "objects of high cultural value or precious art treasures" in the "auction lots of items formerly belonging to the Jew Fromm, Julius" that would be of special interest to the state. In the end there was a net profit of 2,047.80 Reichsmarks.

On this same morning, in this same location, the furniture and the household effects of sixteen other Jewish families that were listed by name were auctioned off, as was the remaining property of an unspecified number of deportees, collectively designated as "O 5205—General," who were evidently so impoverished that the bureaucrats in the finance department did not deem them worthy of individual mention. The yield from the morning's transactions in this single auction house was 25,594.57 Reichsmarks; this money was deposited into the central treasury in Berlin-Brandenburg. From there, the money was transferred to the Reich budget for the 1943 fiscal year, and recorded as "General Administrative Revenues" in Itemized Plan XVII, chapter 7.

These kinds of transactions were the order of the day. For May 21, 1943, the auctioneer Fritz Roth announced in the *Völkischer Beobachter* "on official instructions" that he was selling to the highest bidder—in the same auction rooms that were used for the sale of the Fromms' furniture—"individual pieces of furniture, grand pianos, linens, china, crystal for immediate cash payment." Bernhard Schlüter, a "certified auctioneer for the Greater Berlin area" who resided on Leipziger Strasse, was one of many who catered to discriminating tastes. Also citing "official instructions" that dictated sales to the highest authorized bidder, he was offering "on Tuesday, May 18, at 10 a.m., in his auction rooms at Panoramastr. 1, for immediate cash payment: 1 living room set, 1 bedroom set, 1 child's room set, Biedermeier furniture, corner glass cabinet, rococo suites, individual pieces of furniture, 1 iron fireplace grate, 3 golf bags with clubs, china, crystal, pictures, household effects, etc."

Nowhere near all the loot from the Jewish households was auctioned off, however. A substantial portion was bought up by secondhand and antiques dealers and then offered for sale on the retail market. Other items were sold to privileged individuals with high-priority identification cards, as well as to large families. Victims of bombing raids received preferential treatment from the state, including cash compensation for their losses, which enabled them to stock up on necessities.[72]

In the case of Julius Fromm, fifteen *Volksgenossen* (German national comrades) enjoyed a nice little spending spree. Because the auction on the morning of May 17, 1943, comprised the inventory of additional Jewish households, the proceeds totaled eleven times the amount Fromm's estate yielded. We can therefore infer that on this morning, about eleven times as many Germans, a total of 165, cheerfully and cheaply enhanced their households to the detriment of exiled, deported, and often already murdered Jews. During the war, about five hundred of these kinds of auctions took place in Berlin, so roughly eighty thousand Berliners must have taken part in them. If the proceeds of May 17, 1943, represent an average yield, the auctions of household goods in Berlin alone would have generated additional revenues of 13.5 million Reichsmarks for the state treasury—the equivalent in today's currency of 130 million euros.

Since quite a few of the Fromm household effects were sold in advance directly to Frau Else Bork, and Colonel Hagemann was given the villa, the government revenues and the number of profiteers need to be set significantly higher. But any upward adjustment of the assessment to compensate for these omissions still understates the dimensions of the massive theft, because the truly valuable items do not appear in any sales lists: the Bechstein grand piano in the parlor, the Blüthner piano for the children, the silver dinner set, the holiday china, the large library, the oriental rugs, the crystal chandeliers, the oil paintings, the film projector, the refrigerator, and the cameras. Fromm had had to leave all that behind in Berlin.[73] Evidently there were still others who had lined their pockets handsomely before the official auctions took place, or the objects were appropriated to benefit Nazi luminaries, young artists, officers' clubs, music schools, and the like.

Yet another way to pilfer the property of Jews was to auction off the furniture and clothing that came from the households of the Western European and Czech Jews that had been plundered every which way by the German state. From the occupied western territories alone—France, Belgium, Luxembourg, and the Netherlands—more than 1,300 freight cars transported the household goods of the deported Jews to Berlin. The number of inland ships unloading this kind of freight cannot be determined with any accuracy.[74] Moreover, the clothing of the people who were deported or murdered wound up in secondhand stores or was distributed to the needy by the National Socialist Public Welfare office. If these transactions are factored in, the number of Berliners who profited from the auctions of Jewish property clearly exceeded 200,000. Since most of the profiteers from the deportations at that time were not single households, but rather families of four and five, the number of Berliners whose comfort level increased at the expense of the persecuted and the murdered Jews quickly jumps to a million.

There was something to suit everyone's taste. Even Germans who arrived late or came with an empty wallet and left empty-handed still stood to profit in the end, because the proceeds flowed into the Reich coffers and reduced the tax burden across the board.

The documentation clearly indicates that the Fromms' furniture sold to Colonel Bork and auctioned off to various other buyers had enriched the German state by a total of 4,520.80 Reichsmarks. Despite this evidence, on October 9, 1962, the compensation bureau in Berlin refused once and for all—at least in this case—to make restitution of a single penny for what the civil servants had the audacity to mislabel the "abandonment of furniture."

In contrast to the petitioners, these officials had full access to the original files from the years of Aryanization, which they took advantage of to the detriment of those entitled to restitution. In

Storage facility for "property from Jews" in Oberhausen, ca. 1943

1955, a senior tax collector demanded that the renovations in the Fromms' villa that the tenant, Colonel Hagemann, had insisted on and that had been paid from Fromm's liquid assets "be deducted from the reimbursed sum for the property in the restitution process." Hagemann's air-raid shelter alone must have cost a fortune!

The files also indicate that restitution officials in Berlin were aware of specified assets about which the petitioners had no knowledge. No compensation was made for these assets. For example, Salomon Fromm had taken out a small life insurance policy for his daughter Ruth in 1926, which was to be paid out on February 1, 1944. Payment on maturity had indeed been made—but to the Reich treasury. When in 1958 Ruth Fromm applied for compensation for the losses she and her family had sustained, she did not know about the life insurance policy in her name, and was thus unable to claim restitution, although the administrators knew full well of its existence. They pored through the 1944 correspondence between the life insurance company and the Berlin tax authorities, then added it to their office files—and kept their findings to themselves.

———

At the time of Julius Fromm's formal denaturalization, his personal assets totaled about 1.6 million Reichsmarks, all of which he had to leave behind in the Reich, as we learn from the balance sheet his lawyer, Loebinger, drew up in February 1939.[75] A portion of the proceeds from the sale of his company, in the amount of 300,000 Reichsmarks, should be added to this sum, as should the package of gold and jewelry in the safe deposit box at the Reichs-Kredit-Gesellschaft that Loebinger had not reported as "enemy assets"; this package was easily worth an additional 200,000 Reichsmarks.

The Berlin-Zehlendorf tax office collected 25 percent off the top of the total amount as a "Reich Flight Tax." The cynically named "Jewish atonement payment" of a billion Reichsmarks, which Göring imposed in consultation with the Reich Finance Minister after the November 9 pogrom (Kristallnacht), required every German Jew whose assets exceeded five thousand Reichsmarks to hand over 20 percent of these holdings as a contribution to the German state. Julius Fromm was forced to pay this money, and in addition a "Count Helldorf Donation," named after the Berlin chief of police. This "donation" was extorted from every well-to-do Jewish emigrant from Berlin to augment the municipal treasury. No receipt was issued. Yet another compulsory payment, this one to the Jewish Community in Berlin, was earmarked as poverty aid for Jews of lesser means, who were denied the benefits to which they were entitled as qualifying members of the German social security system, so this money went straight to the German treasury and social security funding as well.

If we add up all these amounts, we find that the government had helped itself to about 50 percent of Fromm's assets by 1939.

The second half was appropriated by the end of 1944. An itemized list of the state's profit from its Aryanization of Fromm's holdings is as follows:

Reich Flight Tax	515,972.00 RM
Jewish Asset Tax	457,770.88 RM
Count Helldorf Donation	50,000.00 RM
Emigration Tax	7,790.00 RM
Reich Railroad Bonds	37,380.00 RM
Account at the Reichs-Kredit-Gesellschaft	14,917.00 RM
Account at the Deutsche Bank	6,181.05 RM
Indemnity for Fromm's sister Else Brandenburg (who was later murdered)	11,456.48 RM
Balance at the Conversion Fund for German Foreign Debts	726.22 RM
Debt Repayment Barth-Probst	4,870.83 RM
Debtor K. Lewis (Mortgage, Impounded)	20,000.00 RM
Debtor K. Lewis (Köpenick), Interest	1,100.00 RM
Debtor Daubitz	30,000.00 RM
Debtor Daubitz, Interest	1,875.00 RM
Debtor Baumann (Coburg)	15,000.00 RM
Debtor Berger (Stralsund)	20,000.00 RM
Debtor Herzka (Dresden)	8,000.00 RM
Debtor Tuphorn	3,466.25 RM
Debtor Tuphorn, Interest	43.12 RM
Debtor Schultz	10,000.00 RM
Remaining Rental Income, Rolandstr.	4,215.01 RM
Sale of Furniture	4,520.80 RM
Sale of Patents	8,802.05 RM
Commerzbank Account	21,361.00 RM
Dresdner Bank Account	123,403.55 RM
Liquid Assets Converted into Reich Treasury Notes, Plus Interest	202,268.20 RM

Additional Interest Payments on the Reich
   Treasury Notes, Paid on June 16, 1943   3,421.25 RM
Residence at Rolandstr. 4 (1919 Purchase Price:
95,000 RM; Minimum Value as of 1933)   300,000.00 RM
Gold and Jewelry Safe Deposit Box at the
   Reichs-Kredit-Gesellschaft   202,320.00 RM
   _____

TOTAL   2,086,860.69

The preceding balance sheet appears to count the sum of the Reich railroad bonds twice (item 5). The restitution process that Ruth Fromm initiated for her father Salomon's expropriated assets indicates the kinds of ploys associated with these bonds. As the Commerzbank advised on May 27, 1955—for a fee of "4 marks for expenses"—it had sold Salomon Fromm's Reich railroad bonds (worth 20,500 Reichsmarks) "in several small units" on the stock exchange. "The final sale of the remaining stocks in the amount of 500 Reichsmarks occurred on November 11, 1940." The proceeds from this sale were immediately converted into war loans and later confiscated.[76] Aside from this item, the nationalization of Julius Fromm's personal assets can be clearly documented.

The above-mentioned sum, which comes close to representing the total figure, should be increased by at least the inheritance tax that Otto Metz-Randa had to pay for Fromms Act in 1941 as the heir of Elisabeth Epenstein, the Aryanizer of the business. The tax office assessed the company's value at 1.9 million Reichsmarks and set the inheritance tax of Metz-Randa, who was not related to the deceased, at 935,000 Reichsmarks.[77] Metz-Randa paid this tax out of the Fromms Act assets.

Factoring in this amount, we discover that a total of about three million Reichsmarks flowed into the Reich treasury and thus to the German *Volksgemeinschaft* (people's community) as a result of the expropriation of Fromm's assets. In today's purchasing power, that would equal about 30 million euros. Elisabeth Epenstein and her heir secured a large portion of the loot for themselves. Others swooped in to profit from the Aryanization on a small or a large scale, notably two high-ranking Wehrmacht officers, who were given manifestly preferential treatment. There was also a covert deal involved in this lucrative transaction for Frau von Epenstein, whereby Göring would get two castles "as gifts" in return for his largesse, and his sisters and a woman identified as "Frau Göring" would receive an allowance for life from the profits of Fromms Act—and did in fact receive this allowance until 1945. Thus the family of a leading Nazi also made money hand over fist.

Julius Fromm had fallen prey to the robbers. These were not a bunch of bandits in the bushes, however, but a state and its citizens. Millions of Germans—Nazis and others—seized the opportunity to profit. According to the principles of social participation, helping the Nazis meant helping themselves. The National Socialist movement may have sprung from an ideological foundation, but it was now fully fused with material interests, thus uniting the Görings, Hagemanns, and Metz-Randas, the men who ran the elevators and the men who ran the country, the tenants in the modest back units and stately front buildings, lower-ranking and top-level officers. Instead of going to a carnival or a sale, everyone happily trotted off to the Jew Auction.

From Villa Fromm to Auschwitz

WHEN ELVIRA FROMM'S HUSBAND, Salomon, and their daughter Ruth fled to England in the spring of 1939, she could not bring herself to accompany them. She was in poor health, and did not want to be financially dependent on her brother-in-law Julius. Above all, she did not want to abandon her only son, Berthold. Berthold had been born with a clubfoot and had failed to measure up to the high academic standards that Salomon had set for him, and was therefore frequently beaten by his father. Many members of this ambitious family separated themselves from its ostensibly weakest link—Berthold. "They always spoke harshly about my brother," Ruth Fromm recalls bitterly.

So Berthold, his mother's fretful problem child, stayed behind with her in Berlin. Until 1939 he earned his living as an optician and precision mechanic in Berlin-Schöneberg. When he was offered the opportunity to escape to Shanghai, he turned it down, because he was afraid of emigrating to the Far East all alone.

———

In 1939 Elvira Fromm moved into the villa on Rolandstrasse, sharing the house with Willy and Else Brandenburg. Before long, though, city officials turned it into a *Judenhaus* (Jew house), and Elvira Fromm and the Brandenburgs were required to take in an elderly widow, Jenny Steinfeld, and a married couple, Wolf and Charlotte Malinowski, who had been forced to vacate their apartments to create more living space for Aryans. In addition, Willy Brandenburg brought his unmarried sister Lisbeth to live with them. Berthold Fromm still had his own apartment at Hohenstaufenstrasse 50, but he visited his mother as often as possible.

None of these people forced to live in such close confines in the Fromm villa left written records of their ordeal. Official files offer our only glimpse into the tragedies that befell them from 1940 to early 1943.

Berthold Fromm, ca. 1940

Berthold Fromm was arrested on November 20, 1941, for undisclosed reasons and brought to Sachsenhausen concentration
camp near Berlin. On May 28, 1942, the civil servant on duty at
the municipal bureau of vital statistics entered the notation: "Shot
on command." He recorded the time of death as seven p.m.[78]
At the noon roll call in the concentration camp, there had
been a sudden order: "Jews, step forward!" Several hundred
prisoners in this category complied, whereupon they were checked
over by an SS commission that had come to the camp for this
express purpose. The elderly, infirm, and frail among them were
separated out; the others, as an SS man put it, "were restored to
life."
All ninety-six of those selected had to go before the firing
squad in the evening in the camp's industrial area. On the same
day, 154 Jewish men—rounded up specifically for this purpose—
suffered the same fate at the same spot, thus adding up to the
specified quota of 250. The mass murder had been carried out
on the orders of Heinrich Himmler. The record of his telephone
calls from May 26 reads: "Jewish hostage execution in retaliation
for the arson attack on the Soviet Paradise exhibit." On May 18,
1942, a resistance group led by the Jewish communist Herbert
Baum had staged an essentially ineffective act of arson at "The
Soviet Paradise," a propaganda exhibit at the Lustgarten in Berlin.[79] In retribution, the SS executed 250 Jewish men by firing
squad, among them the disabled Berthold Fromm. He was twenty-
eight years old.

Lisbeth Brandenburg, born in Kolberg, Pomerania, in 1885, had
been living at Rolandstrasse 4 since November 1941. On July 5,
1942, she was transported to Theresienstadt with the twenty-
second Berlin *Alterstransport*, a transport for the elderly. The Chief

Finance Authority sold the paltry possessions she had left behind ("1 suitcase with underwear and shoes, various items of clothing, lingerie, and table linen") to E. Gartmann, a shop owner in Berlin-Kreuzberg who dealt in secondhand goods, for the price of 219.20 Reichsmarks. Wilhelm Noack, the High Court bailiff, had tallied up the value of these items, but there was still more to be gained for the German war chest from the bank account of Lisbeth Brandenburg. All in all, the national treasury was enriched by 5,638.52 Reichsmarks.[80] Lisbeth Brandenburg died in the concentration camp of Theresienstadt in April 1943.

———

Jenny Steinfeld had to vacate her modest little apartment at Freiherr-vom-Stein-Strasse 6 on September 29, 1941—"with a heavy heart"—and move to a room in the Fromm villa. On the very same day, she drew up her will, and presciently noted that she was "most likely moving to the last place I will ever have on this earth." She stated in the will: "I wish to be cremated and buried in the family tomb in Weissensee."

The daily newspaper *Reichsanzeiger* carried the news of her demise on September 17, 1942, reporting that the assets of "Steinfeld, Jenny Sara" had been "confiscated for the benefit of the German Reich." These assets were fairly substantial. Her family's restitution files encompass thirteen volumes. Born Jenny Blum in 1865, she married Gerhard Steinfeld, a banker in Iława (then Deutsch-Eylau, part of western Prussia), and was widowed in 1915. She was driven to take her own life on August 27, 1942. The Gestapo reported to the Chief Finance Authority: "Steinfeld is a suicide."[81]

Three of her children—Robert, Paul Gerhard, and Ilse Margarete (whose married name was Hamburg)—survived the Holocaust. Her daughter Hertha (whose married name was Birnbaum) was deported to Auschwitz in 1943 and murdered there. In accordance with her last will and testament, Jenny Steinfeld is buried in the Jewish cemetery in Berlin-Weissensee—near the main entrance, at burial ground J1, family tomb # 513.

———

Charlotte Malinowski and her husband, Wolf, an attorney, lived at Am Schlachtensee 38, not far from the Fromms. They, too, had to move to the "Jew house" on Rolandstrasse in 1942. Charlotte Malinowski, née Citron, was born in Berlin in 1890, and Wolf Malinowski was born in 1882 in Pleschen (Pleszew), near Posen (Poznan), which was under Prussian control until 1918. Prior to his deportation, Wolf Malinowski worked as a forced laborer at a company named Daimon in Berlin-Wedding. In late February 1943, the couple were told that they would have to vacate their room on Rolandstrasse. On April 21, the Gestapo informed the Chief Finance Authority: "Charlotte Sara and Wolf Isr. Malinowski, a married couple, are being evacuated shortly. Confiscation instructions to follow." Brückenstein, the court bailiff, inspected the remaining inventory, which was only a small fraction of the assets already "secured" for the state treasury, and set its value at 3,790 Reichsmarks.

On May 18, together with about a thousand other prisoners, the two of them were forced to climb aboard a freight train bound for Auschwitz. They perished there in the gas chambers on the following day—along with more than eight hundred deportees from the same transport.

Willy Brandenburg and his wife, Else, were taken into custody on March 4, 1943. On the questionnaire they were required to fill out in the transit camp, Willy, a former businessman whose company had been taken from him, listed his profession as "worker." He had been forced to work in the Fromms factory in Köpenick for weekly wages of twenty-six Reichsmarks. The same applied to Else, who was paid twenty-three Reichsmarks.

Left to right: Gerhard Fromm with his mother, Anne Fromm, and Willy and Else Brandenburg, ca. 1940

There was evidently method to the madness of making them work in the factory that had so recently been taken away from their brother and brother-in-law. Siegmund Fromm, who had also stayed behind in Berlin, had to perform particularly hard forced labor in that very factory as well. According to witness testimony, the plan was "to humiliate" the family of the former owner by assigning them "the most menial manual labor for a paltry wage."[82] The strategy was meant to highlight the social decline of the former manufacturing family for the permanent staff at Fromms Act, and in doing so would show that the new point of pride was not wealth, but the privilege that comes with lineage in the master race.

———

Elvira Fromm, née Silbergleit, was born in Berlin in 1897. Her husband had left her behind in 1939, her daughter Ruth had emigrated, and her son Berthold had been executed in 1942. Her

Elvira Fromm, ca. 1940

"Aryan" sister-in-law Elsbeth recalled that Elvira remained "unclear about her situation right down to the final days." She lived "only in the hope of being reunited with her relatives" and built "her entire life on this single hope." According to the concierge who lived next door, Elvira Fromm and her in-laws Willy and Else Brandenburg were taken away by the police early on the morning of March 3, 1943, "with nothing but a small bag and a blanket." Afterward, tax officers sealed the doors of the villa—which did not stop neighbors from breaking in and walking off with items they found useful.[83]

On March 6, 1943, Elvira Fromm and the Brandenburgs joined the thirty-fifth *Osttransport*, the transport headed east to Auschwitz. The Chief Finance Authority evidently had an unusual agenda in mind for this transport. The standard procedure was to ship about a thousand people "to the East," but in this case there were 665 people (183 men and 482 women and children). In all probability the idea was for these deportees to move out of attractive apartments that were slated to go to special favorites of the Nazi state as quickly as possible.[84] The train arrived in Auschwitz on the morning of March 7, 1943. One hundred fifty-three men and sixty-five women were assigned to forced labor, and the others perished in the gas chambers the day they arrived; among them were Elvira Fromm and Else and Willy Brandenburg.

———

Once the seven occupants of the Villa Fromm had been evicted and murdered, or were on their way to their deaths, the Hagemanns could settle in comfortably. On April 21, 1943, the Gestapo in Berlin informed the Chief Finance Authority: "The apartment in Berlin-Schlachtensee, Rolandstr. 4, in which the following Jews were living . . . has been allocated by the city planning office in Berlin to Colonel Hagemann, holder of the Knight's Cross. There are no objections to clearing out the apartment."[85] By "clearing out," the Gestapo officers were referring only to the remaining furniture. As described in the previous chapter, it was then auctioned off in May.

The Hagemanns fled from the advancing Red Army in the spring of 1945. The transfer of the house back to the Fromm heirs took place on January 10, 1952. Two years later, they sold it to the mother of the current owner. In 1965 Frau Hagemann rang the doorbell and requested permission to dig in the garden for gold she had previously buried there, particularly a gold statuette of Cupid. She found nothing.

Survival in Paris, London, and Berlin

WHEN FRANCE DECLARED WAR on the German Reich on September 3, 1939, Max Fromm, Julius's eldest son, was interned in Paris as an enemy alien. The actor wound up in a camp named Villerbon, not far from Blois, and lived in fear that in the event of a Wehrmacht attack on France he would fall into the hands of the Gestapo. He therefore volunteered for the Foreign Legion of the French army, which sent him to Morocco. His wife, Paulette, and her mother fled Paris in the chaotic weeks that followed the German invasion in June 1940. They reached Bagnères-de-Bigorre in the Pyrenees, a place that attracted many Jewish refugees because of its proximity to the Spanish border.

In March 1941, Max was discharged from the French army and given enough money to tide him over for two days. The Moroccan authorities, who were under Vichy France control, were now beginning to arrest Jews and hand them over to the Germans. Max and Paulette figured it would be best to flee to Algeria. But Paulette and her mother did not make it over the "green border" (the favored illegal crossing point) to Spain, so Max returned to France. In an attempt to ensure their safety, Paulette forged papers for herself and her husband. She changed their family name Fromm, which was doubly problematic because it sounded both German and Jewish, to Fromin. Supported by wealthy Jews, they lived in a small house in Bagnères-de-Bigorre and were active in the French Resistance, hiding partisans— although they were themselves essentially in hiding. They built a secret trapdoor to enable Resistance fighters to disappear into the cellar.

As the situation in Vichy France became increasingly danger-ous for the Jews, Max Fromm decided to try crossing the border into Spain on his own and continuing on to England, where he would then arrange for Paulette and her mother to join him. On his first attempt, Spanish soldiers caught him and sent him back. For his second attempt, he paid a professional escape agent to bring him over the border on a secure secret route. However, the agent turned out to be cooperating with the Gestapo. Max was arrested and imprisoned in Noé, a camp in Haute-Garonne.

After a few months, he was transferred to a Todt Organization work camp near Marseilles. Along with other forced laborers, he had to build bunkers for the Wehrmacht, to protect the Mediter-ranean coast from a possible Allied invasion. Luckily, his German guards did not discover that there was a Jewish compatriot in the group. Max could not count on keeping his identity secret for long, however. Roll calls to single out circumcised men could occur at any moment. Paulette did everything in her power to save him, and persuaded a group of Resistance fighters to attempt a risky operation. One foggy night, they were able to sneak up to the small camp, knock down the guard, and free Max.

Max, Paulette, and Paulette's mother fled to Tulle, Dordogne, in central France, where Max worked as a charcoal maker in the forest until German units combed through the area in the summer of 1944. Again he wound up in Gestapo custody. His captors were unaware that he was Jewish, and that he spoke German. The prisoners were asked to line up in a row and the Gestapo chief shouted: "Jews, step forward." Max stayed put, understanding full well what his German tormentors were saying about him: "That guy is sure to be a criminal. Let's let him go, and see where he takes off to." They did so, but they soon lost track of him.

At this time, Paulette, who was nearing the end of her first pregnancy, was an inpatient at the local hospital. On June 7, 1944, Resistance partisans, emboldened by the Allied invasion in Normandy, attacked the German occupiers in the town, locked up most of the security regiment in a munitions factory, and liberated Tulle, albeit for just a few short hours. Units of the Second SS Panzer Division Das Reich intervened at once. After they had trounced the Resistance fighters and taken back the city, Brigadier General Heinrich Lammerding ordered ten Frenchmen to be killed for every fallen German.

Max Fromm with the French
Foreign Legion in Morocco, 1940

The SS men rounded up the residents on the market square and forced them to witness the massacre. They hanged ninety-nine prisoners, aged seventeen to forty-five, from balcony lattices, lampposts, and trees. Paulette Fromm later told her son Henri, "On that day, the Germans made widows out of quite a few of the patients in my hospital. They were weeping over their husbands; they were screaming." Paulette feared for Max's safety, but he had found a hiding place in time.

The farther the Allies advanced through northern France, the more the German occupiers' control of the country slipped from their grasp. Max, Paulette, and her mother managed to get to Paris with little Henri, who was born just a few weeks after the massacre at Tulle.

Henri, who is now a psychoanalyst in Paris, gives this sober account of his father: "He was a melancholy man. After the war he never spoke German again, and he was often depressed." Max Fromm traveled to the Federal Republic of Germany a total of three times, and panicked whenever he saw a German in uniform. Friedrich Hollaender, who returned to Munich from Hollywood after the war and performed in a cabaret, offered him a job there. But Paulette and their two sons were French. Max Fromm neither could nor would leave France.

He waited for major film roles to come his way, but he was assigned only bit parts. His main source of income was film dubbing, which he found tedious. In 1949 he was offered a role in *Le Silence de la Mer*, directed by Jean-Pierre Melville, and he later appeared onscreen with Peter Ustinov in Henri-Georges Clouzot's *Les Espions*. Max Fromm played the Gestapo officer in the internationally acclaimed war film *Le Train*. Since he was blond, spoke German, and looked quite Germanic, he was soon typecast as a Nazi, playing Gestapo agents and SS officers. At one point he came close to getting a plum role opposite Brigitte

Bardot, but he was considered too short to be cast with this new star of the French cinema. In 1950 he wrote to a friend from his earlier years in Berlin: "When all is said and done, I have accomplished very little."[86]

Max Fromm never truly considered himself French. German culture remained his spiritual homeland—not Germany per se, his son Henri recalls, but rather the Berlin of the 1920s: "He had achieved a certain degree of fame as an actor there. That was his life, and then it was over."

———

Edgar Fromm, Julius's youngest son, had to report for military duty with the British Pioneers in December 1941. Right from the start, he was asked to adopt a British name—in case he was taken prisoner by the Germans. He refused. The basic military service consisted of digging trenches: "One day, we were digging away as usual when a brigadier general from the War Office and our colonel came by. The brigadier general asked me: "You're not an Englishman, are you?" I said: "No." "What are you then?" "German." He stepped back, and I said, "Sir, you needn't be upset. I am on your side, otherwise I wouldn't be here." He laughed and asked me: "So you speak German?" "Yes, sir. And French, too." Then he turned to our colonel and asked him "Why is this man digging here?" The colonel replied, "He didn't tell me anything about this."

Three weeks later, Edgar Fromm was summoned to the War Office in London. "Two men from the Special Air Service were waiting for me there, dressed in casual clothing; they were smoking cigarettes and looking me over. They figured I could parachute down for espionage missions in France or Germany. I replied: 'I have just gotten married. I'm willing to do anything but that.' They accepted my demurral, and soon I was trained as an interpreter."

Ten days after Allied troops landed in Normandy, Edgar's unit crossed the English Channel, and was caught up in heavy fighting.

*Sergeant Edgar Fromm in
the British Army military
intelligence, 1945*

The unit traveled from Belleville to Brussels. Toward the end of
1944 he first set foot in Germany again, near Aachen, as a sergeant in the military secret service.

Thinking back to his time with the occupying forces, he had
especially vivid memories of a visit to Baroness Thyssen, the wife
of a famous steel magnate. "She wasted no time in declaring: 'I
was never a Nazi.'" "Listen, madam," Edgar Fromm replied, "it
is not my job to determine that. I just need to draw up an inventory of your possessions." When he returned from this mission,
a fellow British officer asked him, "Did you bring home a nice
souvenir?" The otherwise amiable Edgar Fromm seethed with
indignation as he replied, "The Nazis did that to us, and that is
exactly why I will not do so!"

Edgar Fromm never felt hatred for the Germans—perhaps because most members of his family survived the Holocaust. In contrast to many of his Jewish refugee friends in London, he traveled

to his native country on a regular basis. He even toyed with the idea of moving back to Germany, but his wife, whose parents had been murdered in German death camps, balked at the thought of doing so. "I felt rather sorry for most Germans after the war," Edgar Fromm said. "They went along with their holy Führer and paid such a heavy price for having done so."

———

Ruth Fromm likewise insists: "I do not hate the Germans. Even so, I no longer think of myself as German, although I did grow up in Berlin." Just after the war ended, she signed on with the United States Army, which needed a large number of bilingual staff members. On the way from England to Germany, she sought and found her cousin Max, his wife Paulette, and their son Henri, who had just turned one. The family was living in Paris "in appalling conditions." Her next stop was Munich, where, she recalls, "They fired shots at us. The people of Munich did not like the Americans at all, and thought the British had started the war."

In Nuremberg she translated documents, including descriptions of experiments on humans that had been conducted in Auschwitz on behalf of I.G. Farben, for use in the criminal trials. She had the impression, though, that the investigative and prosecutorial zeal demonstrated in the first spectacular trial took a nosedive in subsequent efforts to prosecute Nazi criminals. The case of Göring, one of the men sentenced to death, wound up casting suspicion on her and her American coworkers. When Hermann Göring poisoned himself, they were accused of having helped him get hold of the cyanide. American soldiers had taken Göring into custody on May 9, 1945, at his castle, Mauterndorf. Before they led him away, this man, who had profited most from the Aryanization of Fromms Act, summed up his feelings about National Socialism in this matter-of-fact statement: "At least I lived a decent life for twelve years."

After working with National Socialist files in Nuremberg for six months, Ruth Fromm had had quite enough, and applied for a transfer to Berlin. In the demolished city of her birth, she tracked down her uncle Siegmund and her cousin Gerhard, the son of Alex, who had fled to London. She brought Siegmund and his family food from PX stores, which were restricted to U.S. military personnel. Gerhard, who had just been liberated from years of racial persecution, could not accept the fact that Ruth was working for the American occupiers. He and his wife, who had lived in the Fromm villa at one point, now returned to the house, and discovered that old family photographs were still in the basement. A concierge in a neighboring building recalled the day that Ruth's mother, her aunt, and her aunt's husband had been taken away. Ruth's father, Salomon, was shattered by this news.

Salomon Fromm died on February 19, 1947, in London. He lies buried in a northwestern suburb of the city. His tombstone

Ruth Fromm in the U.S. Army, 1947

carries the English-language inscription: "Also in memory of his wife and son Ella Fromm and Berthold Fromm, who both suffered death in German concentration camps."

———

Siegmund was the only one of Julius Fromm's brothers and sisters to have survived National Socialism and the war while remaining in Berlin. A joint owner of Fromms Cosmetics, Siegmund had spent a long time weighing the pros and cons of fleeing to England, but he was quite attached to his charming apartment in Berlin. By the time Germany started the war, it was too late. His wife, Elsbeth, was "of German blood," but had converted to Judaism before the wedding. In 1932 she gave birth to Alfred. A year later, she converted back to Christianity, and was classified as an Aryan. She also had Alfred baptized in May 1943. Even so, the authorities in Berlin labeled him a *Geltungsjude* (legal equivalent of a Jew), because of his Jewish religious instruction, and forced him to wear a yellow star.

Helene, Siegmund, and Elsbeth Fromm in Berlin, 1947

The four weeks Siegmund spent in the Sachsenhausen concentration camp took a severe toll on his health. After his release in late 1938 he was required to report to the police daily for a full year. "Only someone who has experienced this," he wrote in November 1945, "can appreciate what it means." After the attacks on Poland and the Soviet Union, he was imprisoned in the police headquarters at Alexanderplatz, and suffered a mild "tension-induced stroke." In March 1943, he was again taken into temporary custody, this time on Rosenstrasse. "This is why I often stayed away from my apartment for days or even weeks on end."

His wife, Elsbeth, was "put to work as a washerwoman at Bergmann Company laundering soldiers' coats, on orders from the Gestapo." She contracted jaundice. Siegmund was no better suited for a prolonged period of hard labor, and he suffered "a complete physical and mental breakdown." Beginning in 1942, he was forced

Alfred Fromm, foreground center, with the Schmidts, who hid him, summer 1944; his mother, Elsbeth Fromm, is behind him to the right

to work as a packer for a printing press. "We watched him wither away with each passing day," Elsbeth recalls.

Sunniva Graefe, a Finnish woman who had moved into Paulsborner Strasse 8 in Berlin-Wilmersdorf in 1941, struck up a friendship with the couple. To "declare [her] solidarity" with them and their son, Alfred, she accompanied them "into the special air-raid shelter for Jews." She, too, watched "Herr Fromm grow more nervous by the day." He had "crying fits," and "later [gave] the impression of a man who was deeply tormented, both physically and mentally." He died in 1952 at the age of fifty-nine.

Alfred often played with the two sons of Max Schmidt, a shoe-maker who lived nearby on Paulsborner Strasse. As the air strikes grew ever more intense, the Schmidts decided in early 1943 to move to their house near Balz-Süd, in the vicinity of Landsberg on the Warta River. Gertrud Schmidt, a warmhearted

Alfred Fromm's future wife,
Ilse Haacke, ca. 1945

working-class woman from Berlin, liked Alfred and understood the danger he faced in having to wear a yellow star, so she passed him off as her son, and took him with her to the country. He had to hide in the barn whenever there were visitors. However, he was quite a bit safer there than in Berlin. The eleven-year-old boy wrote to his mother in the spring of 1943: "I wish you a happy birthday and hope you are not bothered by any air-raid sirens. Too bad I wasn't able to come."[87]

Only once, in the summer of 1944, did Elsbeth Fromm dare to visit her son. Late in January 1945, Alfred set off alone for Berlin. The roar of gunfire on the front could be heard on the night that the boy, who had just turned thirteen, joined the refugees heading west. He and two German soldiers crossed the Oder River, which had frozen over. After stealing a uniform jacket from a boy in the Hitler Youth and discovering valid papers in it, he managed to find his way to his parents in Berlin. Alfred Fromm wrote an autobiographical account of this experience in 1996, and recalled the moment of liberation: "On May 1, 1945, at about 8 p.m., Red Army soldiers liberated us. When they came into our cellar, I hugged and kissed them, one after the other."

He later married Ilse Haacke, a Jewish woman from Berlin. Before being deported to Theresienstadt, her mother had brought Ilse to stay with the Christian adoptive parents of her husband's second wife in southern Germany. They passed her off as an "Aryan," and in this way she was able to survive the Holocaust. Today she is a widow living in Munich. She shudders at the memory of having to make coffee for SS men in Bavaria: "We were both traumatized as children," Ilse Fromm recalls, "and we were plagued by complexes. We always had the feeling that we were worthless. Alfred suffered from anxiety his whole life. It would have been better if our parents had not brought us into this world."

"PROPERTY OF THE PEOPLE" IN THE NEW GERMANY

THE MACHINES THAT PRODUCE CONDOMS TODAY are called chains. Three of these production chains, each over a hundred feet long, turn out condoms bearing the brand name Fromms FF in a factory in the industrial zone of Zeven, situated between Hamburg and Bremen. The MAPA manufacturing company is part of Total, a multinational energy company based in France. With a market share of over 13 percent in 2005, Fromms ranks as the brand with the second-highest sales of condoms in Germany.

A pungent odor of ammonia suffuses the production area. Adding ammonia to the latex prevents curdling during shipping from Malaysia to Germany. For about ten days, the latex, enhanced with all kinds of undisclosed additives, undergoes a swelling process in Zeven, and is then ready to be placed on one of the chains, each of which holds approximately one thousand glass molds, commonly called mandrels, mounted at intervals of 2.75 inches. In 1995 a European norm (EN 600) was introduced to standardize condom sizes at 6.69 inches in length and 1.8 to 2.2 inches in diameter.

The glass mandrels are cleaned in a tank, then dried and drawn—one by one—through a small basin filled with milky latex. A thin (0.0011-inch), virtually transparent coating adheres to the mandrels. Then the chain runs through a drying chamber, and a second round of dipping and drying follows, after which brushes roll up the open ends of the raw condoms to form a rim. Once the condoms have been sprayed off the mandrels with high-pressure jets of water, they are placed in large washing machines, where denatured cornstarch is added. Then the condoms dry at 140 to 194 degrees Fahrenheit, and undergo quality testing. Only two condoms are inflated per hour. They have to be able to hold at least 4.75 gallons of air before bursting; many can take in more than 13 gallons. Individual testing with air has now been replaced by quality control using electrical current. Each condom is mounted onto a metal form and rotates between two rods charged at two thousand volts. If the condom has a hole or a thin area, the current passes through, and the defective item falls into a container for rejects.

Like so many twenty-first-century factories, the hall is eerily devoid of a human presence. One worker monitors the computers that control the chain, and loads the washing machines and dryers. A second worker places the condoms on the testing equipment, which has yet to be fully automated. In the course of three shifts, six workers produce about a hundred thousand condoms. A staff of twenty-eight manufactures an annual total of about 80 million units.

In the 1960s, the benzene process Julius Fromm had employed was discontinued and replaced by a new latex-manufacturing process. Apart from that innovation, and an increasing degree of automation, the technology has remained unchanged.

———

Condom production in Zeven began in the summer of 1947. At that time, Hannes Bachmann, a businessman in Bremen, and

Bruno Engelhardt, a former chief executive at a rubber factory in Hildesheim, decided to form a company to produce rubber products. Bachmann and Engelhardt intended to center their business on manufacturing waterproof aprons. They applied to the British military administration in Hanover for permission, but were turned down for this product. The occupying forces were troubled by the steadily rising number of cases of venereal disease after the end of the war, and by the fact that both the Fromms Act factories (in East Berlin) and the Blausiegel factories (in Erfurt and Leipzig) were part of the Soviet zone. The British wanted an independent condom factory to provide this necessary product for the three Western zones.

The two businessmen lacked any experience in condom production, but a lucky coincidence brought them in contact with a former production manager at Fromms Act when they attended the first postwar Leipzig Trade Fair. This production manager was

Production of the FF Fromm brand of condoms in Zeven, 2006

looking for work, and had the expertise and professional experience they were seeking.

Bachmann and Co. Hanseatic Rubber Factory, Inc., was granted an operating license by the British military government on October 1, 1947. The industrial site near Zeven, where a large army munitions factory had just been dismantled, was well suited for use as a production plant. This factory, referred to as the Muna, had been making artillery shells and mortar bombs for the Wehrmacht since 1940—increasingly by Soviet prisoners of war.

Since the factory lay well-camouflaged in a dense forest, the buildings as well as the electrical and water supplies had remained intact during the war. A workforce could be assembled readily from the refugees from Germany's eastern territories. The bigger challenge was to acquire the requisite machinery. As luck would have it, Engelhardt, the cofounder of the company, had run a large rubber factory in Lodz during the war, and as the Soviet troops were advancing, he dismantled a rolling mill for rubber and brought it to the West. This looted machine would come in quite handy.

Production in Zeven began in December 1948, with male workers' wages set at seventy-eight pfennigs an hour. Women were paid hourly wages of fifty-two pfennigs. In 1991 *Gummilinse* (Rubber Lens), the company newsletter, ran a piece recalling the "enormous and now-unthinkable" benzene fumes that plagued the workers, and the "horrid, back-breaking work . . . of setting up the dipping frames" on which the glass mandrels were mounted. Many workers developed tendinitis.

The quality of the product was also erratic. Reject rates approached 8 percent, and a trade show for hairdressers in Bremen turned out disastrously for the inexperienced condom manufacturers. A chronicle of the company's history tells the story of a prospective buyer who suddenly showed up at the booth, "filled a condom with water right in front of everyone, and the water poured out in a steady stream, making the condom look like a watering can."[88]

At this point, the former plant manager from Fromms Act tracked down Herbert and Edgar Fromm in London, who had also opened a small condom factory there, and proposed a license agreement. The old familiar trademark, they reasoned, could help them on the road to glory. Herbert and Edgar Fromm gave their consent, since they were facing overwhelming competition from London Rubber's Durex condoms in Great Britain. In January 1949, they signed a mutually beneficial twenty-five-year license agreement with the Hanseatic Rubber Company.

———

The only problem was that the sons and heirs of Julius Fromm no longer owned the trademark. Fromms Act in Berlin, which, since the death of Elisabeth Epenstein, had belonged to her heir, Otto Metz-Randa, now held the rights to this brand name. Metz-Randa, using the fact that he was from Vienna to his advantage, quickly transformed himself from a pan-German profiteer of Aryanization into a persecuted Austrian, a paragon of innocence. He even tried to pass himself off as a victim of National Socialist tyranny.

Bachmann, the founder of the postwar incarnation of the company, traveled to Vienna with Sally Jaffa, Julius Fromm's old attorney in Berlin, who had survived the war in London, to meet with Metz-Randa. Edgar Fromm recalled that Metz-Randa "was fully expecting to hear from us." The Demographics Division of the Municipal Administration of Vienna now listed Metz-Randa as a retiree, but he saw—and seized—his chance yet again to reap a handsome profit from his shady inheritance.

Metz-Randa refused to hand over the company and the trademark. He contacted the "Trustees of the American, British, and

French Military Government for Assets Transferred Under Duress" to contest the Fromm brothers' demands. Metz-Randa argued that "because the sales contract at that time was not in the nature of a 'forced contract,'" the claim was "not defensible." This was the brazen argument of a Viennese businessman in 1951, whose role in Elisabeth Epenstein's life, first as her consultant and then as her heir, had enabled him to take over at least three formerly Jewish companies (Fromms Act, Fromms Cosmetics, and a castle hotel plus estate in Gösing in Lower Austria).

Otto Metz-Randa instructed Walter Fuhrmann, an attorney and notary public in Berlin, to put a stop to any possible return of the company to the Fromm family. Fuhrmann characterized the sale of Fromms Act to Elisabeth Epenstein as "a transaction completed for purely financial reasons [and] unrelated to the Nazi regime." He claimed that Fromm had "already decided in 1933" to emigrate, and he sold his company "so that he could enhance the new life he had already begun to build abroad, that is, in En-

Testing Fromms condoms in Zeven, 1965

gland." The attorney also reported that there had been other offers to buy the company, including an offer by a "German Briton named Koch." He alleged that "of all these bids [Fromm] favored the one from . . . Frau v. Epenstein."

The attorney representing Fromm's sons in Bremen vehemently denied this allegation. Fuhrmann fired back by speculating that "it appears absolutely out of the question that the seller—if he were still alive—would have made claims for restitution." On top of that, he explained that "special directives from the Reich Marshal's chief of staff had granted extraordinary currency and transfer relief far exceeding those in any other case."

In the summer of 1951, after several months of this wrangling, Fromm's sons realized that they would be forced to agree to a settlement, and signed the papers with Metz-Randa after driving a hard bargain at the forty-fourth restitution tribunal of the district court in Berlin. The settlement stipulated that Metz-Randa, the consultant to and heir of the Aryanizer Elisabeth Epenstein, would transfer his share of the business to them. In return, the heirs of Julius Fromm, who had been stripped of his company, would remit the "sum total of 174,300 West German Marks" to Metz-Randa.[89] At the time of this settlement, which came so soon after the war and the currency reform, this was an astronomical sum of money.

———

When the Hanseatic Rubber Company set about advertising its condoms, the emphasis was on their protective function. The first advertising brochure, "Sun of Life, Health of the People," cited statistics on the increase in gonorrhea and syphilis, and provided this explanation: "An uncertain past" that posed "obscure perils" had made "many people go the way of folly" and "become reckless," making them "a danger to people today in the truest sense of the word."

The product line also included "tried and true" Fromms rubber sponges and hot-water bottles. The following pointer was intended to reassure buyers of condoms: "Fromms has come to stand for this kind of prophylactic, and its name is a guarantee that you are getting the very best. You should insist on Fromms, and make it clear that you will accept only genuine Fromms products from the Western occupation zones."[90] The key message here is "Western," with its suggestion of quality inherently superior to products manufactured in East Berlin.

————

The Fromms factory in Köpenick was nearly obliterated by bombs on December 24, 1943, and on January 17, 1945, days on which the Allied air force launched strategic and highly effective attacks on the entire German rubber industry.[91] On April 23, 1945, the Red Army marched into Köpenick. One day later, Berthold Viert and Karl Lewis, the two long-term directors of Fromms Act, committed suicide. The motives behind their decision to end their lives remain a mystery. However, their despicable treatment of the three Fromm family members who were forced to work in the factory would seem to suggest that they had less to fear from the Soviet soldiers than from the return of their former boss.

The machines that had remained intact through the air strikes were immediately dismantled and shipped to the Soviet Union.[92] By contrast, the older factory in Friedrichshagen, which had survived essentially undamaged, was readied for operation to supply the Red Army soldiers with condoms immediately needed. On orders from the Soviet military commander of the city, Fromms Act's head chemist, Dr. Wilfried Genth, got the factory up and running again just seven weeks after the capitulation of the German Reich. Raw materials were on hand, and, according to a report submitted by the industrial union Chemicals, Paper, Stones, and Earth on July 15, 1946, "the Russians bought our products without delay."

The author of this text was Reinhold Schobert, the head of the staff association at Fromms Act, who had been appointed by the Friedrichshagen employment office. In this report he expressed his views about Dr. Genth and Genth's girlfriend Elisabeth Lipova. "Genth," Schobert wrote, "and his assistant, Fräulein Lipova, a Polish woman, [acted] as though the company belonged to them, and as though nothing whatsoever had happened in Germany." Unfortunately, Schobert explained, Genth's position was unassailable, "because the Russians have opened a testing division with us ... and the Polish woman, Lipova, is assisting him." This "Polish woman" was actually a Czech woman who had been deported to Germany in 1941 as a forced laborer. Schobert, an unelected proletarian functionary who had not been active in the company since he was fired in 1933, until his appointment as head of the staff association, vented his frustration in this report: "I cannot get it through my thick worker's skull how something like this is possible in a free Germany; it is as though a person were irreplaceable." Not so very long ago, this same worker's skull had belonged to a Nazi Party official. In this regard, he was not so very different from Genth, who had become a member of the Nazi Party in 1933.

According to the regulations of the Potsdam Agreement, Julius Fromm or his heirs, as victims of the Nazi dictatorship, should have had the factories in Berlin-Köpenick and Friedrichshagen returned to them. In September 1945, the district court judge in charge of the Berlin company register confirmed that "in view of the political constellation ... Herr Julius Fromm is to be reinstated as the true owner." But the German communists in the Soviet zone (and then in the German Democratic Republic) prevented this from happening.

The district office in Berlin-Köpenick began by putting the Köpenick factory premises and buildings under trustee administration. It then registered the real estate with the Soviet Military Administration (SMAD) as "unclaimed property" and delegated it to the Köpenick district authority. The SMAD handed over both the company and the factory in Friedrichshagen to the district office for trustee administration. Siegmund Fromm fought in vain to "reinstate" Julius Fromm's previous "rights as the sole proprietor of Fromms Act Rubber Company, Inc."

———

Late in March 1946, the company was placed into forced administration, and, three years later, nationalized by the German Trustee Administration for the benefit of the German Democratic Republic in accordance with Edict 124. The bureaucrats did not follow the letter of the law, however, as the ukase issued in October 1945 by Marshal Zhukov of the Red Army provided only for the takeover of property from "chief officers" and "leading members and supporters" of the Nazi Party. The Fromm family plainly did not fall into this category.[93]

The East Berlin officials were well aware of this. To be on the safe side, they made out Julius Fromm, the inventor and founder of the company, to be a capitalist villain. A 1948 document describing this case contains the following remarks, under the heading "Incriminating Evidence":

I. Jewish proprietor, capitalist exploiter, antisocial, anti-labor, and pro-Nazi views. . . . Although a Jew himself, J. Fromm—and all parties concur on this point—was one of those capitalist exploiters who used all means and methods at his disposal, in the most unscrupulous manner, to maximize his profit at the expense of others. The primitive production facilities and antiquated or in some cases nonexistent hygienic and other requisite amenities at the plant in Friedrichshagen took a heavy toll on the workforce as a whole, and on the health of the workers employed there. The "savings" he hoped to achieve were coupled with the worst possible piecework wages, which bore no relation to the prices they commanded, and in just a few short years gave him the financial foundation he needed to construct the factory in Köpenick (1930—turn key price, ca. 6 million marks).

There was no denying that Julius Fromm had "developed and expanded the various amenities in the company." These changes were now being used against him as "incriminating evidence" of his "active support of National Socialist propaganda." To add insult to injury, the report also claimed that Fromm had sold his company of his own free will and that he had gone so far as to target the sale to "a reactionary buyer [Göring's godmother] to make a lucrative foreign currency transaction."

Sworn statements by four men corroborated this "incriminating evidence." One of them, Schobert, had written the vitriolic attack against the chemist Genth and the supposedly Polish woman Elisabeth Lipova two years earlier. The four men characterized themselves as antifascists. However, they had been defeated in the workers' council elections in October 1946, "because," they explained, "the elections came too early for a company of this kind." On January 17, 1948, the activists gave more evidence to boost their claim: "The Fromm family brought a large portion of their assets and merchandise to England even before 1933, and when they boarded a plane and flew to England, they weren't bothered in the least about what was happening to their workers." In July 1948, Schobert's brother-in-law Herzog added: "The Jewish owner, Julius Fromm, was an exploiter of the worst sort, utterly lacking in any understanding of social responsibility." All four regarded their former boss as "nothing but a capitalist," and they declared: "We cannot stand this sort of person, which is why these companies belong in the hands of the people."

An administrative report about the Fromms company that Nazi officials had drawn up in 1934 while preparing to strip Julius

Fromm of his citizenship told a very different story: "Most of the workers are paid more than the standard rate" and "the staff facilities are impeccable; all the workrooms are equipped with adequate ventilation, and with heating in the winter and cooling in the summer. Washrooms and showering facilities are available to the workers." This report also noted that Fromm provided for the physical well-being of his employees by making lunch—"soup, meat dish, and stewed fruit"—available at a bargain price.[94]

However, the German trusteeship was not receptive to these points when considering the case in October 1948. Instead, it incorporated the distinctly anti-Semitic tirades of the workers' representatives nearly verbatim into its "recommendation for transfer to state ownership." The "incriminating evidence" evolved into "incriminating facts" that emphasized Fromm's "anti-humanitarian and anti-labor attitude." The explanation ran as follows: "After 1933, the attack on the staff was stepped up, in an evident attempt by the Jewish company to ingratiate itself with the Nazi regime."

One year later, on December 2, 1949, officials in the newly established German Democratic Republic completed the final steps in the nationalization process. The journal of administrative orders for Greater Berlin announced: "In light of the law of February 8, 1949, confiscating property assets of war criminals and Nazi activists, the city council of Greater Berlin has resolved to confiscate without compensation the property assets of the individuals and companies noted in List 3 below as assets of war criminals and Nazi activists and to transfer them to ownership by the people." The text for reference no. 133 read: "Fromms Act Rubber Company, Inc., Berlin-Friedrichshagen, Rahnsdorfer Str. 153."

The notice was signed by Friedrich Ebert, the son of the late president of the Weimar Republic. Ebert, a former member of the

Social Democratic Party, was now serving on the Central Committee of the Socialist Unity Party of Germany, and was the mayor of Greater Berlin. On June 24, 1951, the factory was formally entered in the land registry as "property of the people." KAUTAS (United People's Factories for Rubber and Asbestos) manufactured condoms there until the end of the 1950s.

Later on, "Fromms Act—made of pure natural rubber—luxury" was produced by People's Enterprise Plastina in Erfurt, at the nationalized Richter and Käufer Rubber Factories (formerly Blausiegel). The cost of a three-pack was 1.25 East German marks. Just as in the old days, a coupon printed on the packets that could be slid unobtrusively over the drugstore counter came with these instructions: "Please use this slip of paper for discreet purchases at your specialty store." Eventually the Fromms brand was renamed Mondos, and this name became synonymous with condoms in the German Democratic Republic.

————

Condemned to idleness during World War II, Julius Fromm wavered between depression and hope. On good days in his exile in London, he dreamed of rebuilding the company that had been stolen from him. Shortly before the defeat of Hitler's Germany, he drew up a will "in regard to my assets in Germany and Danzig," which sketched out two possible outcomes, one entailing reacquisition of the factories, and the other financial restitution. In any case, he made his sons promise to do everything in their power to save the business, and to entrust an "impartial arbitrator" to resolve any disputes about the inheritance that might arise.

The extent to which Julius Fromm retained his faith in the German people and their respect for justice and for upstanding citizens like himself is revealed in a clause that established how the impartial arbitrator was to be appointed, should his sons disagree even on this point. Fromm wrote in his will in December

*Julius Fromm shortly before
his death in England*

1944 that the arbitrator "should be chosen by the president of the Berlin chamber of commerce." And of course it was Berlin that he had in mind when he wrote to his son Max in liberated France on February 6, 1945: "As soon as the war is over, I will begin again."[95]

That is not how things turned out. On May 12, 1945, three days after hundreds of thousands of people had exuberantly celebrated victory on London's Trafalgar Square and in front of Buckingham Palace, Julius Fromm got up in the morning, and when he tried to open the curtains, he collapsed. The doctor was hurriedly summoned, but by the time he arrived, the patient had died.

Julius Fromm's heart had given out, his family said, because he had been so overjoyed about the demise of the Nazis and the prospect of his imminent return to Germany.

Large-handed robbers thy grave masters are,
And pill by law.

—SHAKESPEARE, *Timon of Athens*

FOR THE GENERATION of Julius Fromm's grandchildren, born shortly after the war in the freedom and democracy of Great Britain and France and lucky enough not to have had to endure the Nazi years, Michael Sontheimer and Götz Aly's work has been a real eye-opener. We naturally got to hear quite a lot through our fathers about the origins and achievements of our relatives, particularly their father, Julius Fromm, but this was mostly anecdotal. So we knew relatively few details about our forebears' past. One must not forget that—as with many others who lived though the years of National Socialism—it was incredibly distressing for our parents to talk about their experiences. My mother, too, a German Jewess who came to England alone and practically penniless from Hamburg in March 1939, very seldom spoke about her parents, particularly about her mother, who was murdered in Auschwitz in 1943. It was just too traumatic!

As a result, it has also mostly been too painful for my generation to think about what happened before we were born. Finding it easier and more practical to leave the past to our parents' generation, we threw ourselves into the modern world, into the present day of a new, more peaceful, and freer Europe. For these reasons, we asked our parents far too little about the Nazi times and thus never learned the details of what had occurred.

It is only as one gets older, however, and one's parents pass away that one begins to reflect more about the past. One wants to know what happened to relatives, how they fared in the period of assimilation of prewar Germany, how their lives and activities were suddenly shattered through persecution, what suffering they had to endure and what finally happened to them. With our parents gone, though, whom should we ask and where should we begin?

A stroke of good fortune then befell the Fromm family through its connection to Michael Sontheimer. He had always retained a fascination for our family's history and had for a long time harbored a desire to write a book about it one day. Further luck and events conspired that he would eventually team up with Götz Aly. As a result of their trawling through the archives in Germany and even in Poland, the Fromm family's original native country, a detailed story began to emerge, considerably more accurate in detail than what the postwar Fromm generation knew. It falls to me to express the whole Fromm family's heartfelt thanks to Michael Sontheimer and Götz Aly for their undertaking. Without their efforts, none of what had long since drifted into oblivion would ever have been brought back to life, nor as my late father, Edgar Fromm, once requested of Michael Sontheimer, would the name of his inventive father, Julius, ever have been put back on the map.

Some people have asked me what the purpose of this book is: indeed, should one not rather leave the past well alone? I personally cannot subscribe to this view, since this book has a much wider purpose than simply relating another tale of persecution and Holocaust, for it serves as an example of the fate that befell not only the Fromm family but those of countless other German and Continental Jewish families. These families may perhaps not have been as rich and successful as Julius Fromm but, in the end, the huge, corrupt looting carried out by the Nazis affected all German and Continental Jewish families in one way or another. Consequently, my generation of children of Continental European Jewish parentage have very few items to remind us of the past. This does not necessarily mean a family heirloom of financial value, but mementos from the past—indeed from our family's *German* past. And in some cases this past was very German: for example, on my mother's side I can trace our family back over six centuries, generation after generation, seventeen in all, having lived their lives in Germany until the Holocaust. From her family in Hamburg as well as from my wife's maternal family, also from Hamburg, only very few heirlooms remain because very little could—or was allowed to—be taken into emigration and what remained behind was subsequently stolen, never to be returned. Moreover—quite apart from many items never having been restored, let alone compensated for—where it proved possible after the war to lodge legal claims for documented expropriated assets, the amounts reimbursed bit by bit over the decades have, for the most part, been but a small fraction of their original worth. Indeed, some documented assets have to this day never been restituted. All this has, alas, served only to perpetuate the legalized theft that resulted from Aryanization.

In his well-known book about German Jewry entitled *The Pity of It All*, the Israeli author Amos Elon describes how the assimilation of German Jews began in 1743 with the immigration to Berlin of the famous German-Jewish philosopher Moses Mendelssohn, the founder of Jewish Enlightenment, who entered the Prussian capital through the city gate reserved for cattle and Jews. That story of a noble experiment to assimilate came tragically full circle almost two hundred years later, when hundreds of thousands of German Jews were deported to meet their deaths in the extermination camps in railway trucks—equally designated for cattle and Jews. The poignant symmetry here is as shocking as it is painful. For a period of almost two centuries, most Jews living in Germany tried very hard to assimilate into the German lifestyle. They succeeded, their assimilation blossoming and flourishing during this era and contributing symbiotically to a substantial enrichment of German culture, science, and commerce. That this attempt went so sadly awry and ended in tears is the tragedy not only of our family but that of all German Jewry. Even today, sixty-four years after the end of the Third Reich, we of German-Jewish descent still feel the demise of German Jewry to be not only a great sorrow, but also an unbelievable tragedy and pity.

All of us in the Fromm family hope that, through their detailed account of our family's story as victims of state-organized plunder, the authors' sterling work will serve to support George Santayana's wise warning that those who forget the past are condemned to repeat it. It is our sincere wish that this informative, enlightening book will find its niche in the vast library of volumes about the Third Reich so that from it, too, among the many others, the lessons from the past can be learned and thus a repetition of the appalling errors from history may be avoided.

London, January 2009

Baruch Fromm, known as *Bernhard*, born on October 10, 1854, in Konin (Russia), died on June 18, 1898, in Berlin; married to *Sara Rifka Fromm*, née Riegel, known as *Regina*, born on January 24, 1859, in Konin, died on July 13, 1911, in Berlin. Their marriage produced eight children:

1. *Szlama Fromm*, known as *Salomon* or *Sally*, born on November 27, 1880, in Konin, died on February 19, 1947, in London; married to *Elvira Fromm*, née Silbergleit, born on July 16, 1887, in Berlin, murdered on March 7, 1943, in the Auschwitz concentration camp. Their marriage produced two children:
    1.1 *Berthold Fromm*, born on May 29, 1914, in Berlin, shot dead on May 28, 1942, in the Sachsenhausen concentration camp.
    1.2 *Ruth Fromm*, born on May 10, 1920, in Berlin, lives in New York.

2. *Israel Fromm*, known as *Julius*, born on March 4, 1883, in Konin, died on May 12, 1945, in London; married to *Selma Fromm*, née Lieders, born on October 6, 1881, in Berlin, died on April 21, 1946, in London. Their marriage produced three sons:

2.1 *Max Fromm,* born on April 21, 1907, in Berlin, died on December 27, 1969, in Paris; married to *Paulette Fromm,* née Fromm (daughter of Hermann Fromm, a cousin of Julius Fromm from Konin), born on October 16, 1906, in Paris, died on August 12, 2000, in Paris. Their marriage produced two children: *Henri-Jean* and *Julien Fromm,* who live in Paris and Segny, respectively.

2.2 *Herbert Fromm,* born on June 27, 1911, in Berlin, died on November 22, 1961, in Bremen; married to *Ellen Rose Fromm,* née Friedländer, born on June 10, 1914, in Berlin, died on May 17, 2004, in Zurich.

2.3 *Edgar Fromm,* born on October 26, 1919, in Berlin, died on June 19, 1999, in Bühl in Baden; married to *Jolanthe Fromm,* née Wolff, born on February 16, 1911, in Hamburg, died on August 10, 1979, in Flims (Switzerland). Their marriage produced *Raymond Fromm,* who lives in London.

3. *Mosziek (Moses) Fromm,* known as *Max,* born on April 15, 1885, in Konin, died on December 18, 1930, in Berlin; married to *Selma Fromm,* née Wolff, died in Johannesburg (South Africa). Their marriage produced:

3.1 *Rolf Rudi Fromm,* born on June 21, 1912, in Berlin, died in 2003 in Johannesburg; married to *Anna Fromm,* born on July 20, 1914, died on June 4, 1990, in Johannesburg.

4. *Helene Fromm,* born on February 12, 1887, in Konin, died on February 11, 1952, in London; briefly married in Berlin to a cousin on her mother's side named Riegel (Rygel).

5. *Siegmund Fromm,* born on May 1, 1890 in Konin, died on September 1, 1952 in Berlin; married to *Elsbeth Fromm,* née Kuntze, a Protestant woman who converted to Judaism, born on May 14, 1897, in Berlin, died there on October 16, 1992. Their marriage produced:

5.1 *Alfred Fromm,* born on April 11, 1932, in Berlin, died on July 6, 2002, in Munich; married to *Ilse Fromm,* née Haacke, born on March 29, 1929, in Cottbus (Germany), lives in Munich.

6. *Esther Fromm,* known as *Else,* born on September 5, 1893, in Konin, married to *Willy Brandenburg,* born on June 25, 1890, in Kolberg; both were murdered in the Auschwitz concentration camp on March 7, 1943. Their marriage produced:

6.1 *Bruno Brandenburg,* born on June 25, 1918, in Breslau, died on July 18, 1928, in Berlin.

7. *Sander Fromm,* known as *Alexander* or *Alex,* born on August 3, 1895, in Berlin, died on March 6, 1957, in London; married to a Christian woman, *Anna Fromm,* née Machnik, born on January 7, 1893, in Wissek/Schneidemühl, died on October 8, 1972, in London. Their marriage produced:

7.1 *Gerhard Fromm,* born on October 22, 1920, in Berlin, died there on August 7, 1998; married to *Liselotte Fromm,* née Fiebig, born on December 15, 1916, in Berlin, died there on November 6, 1987. Their marriage produced *Michael Fromm,* who lives in Berlin.

8. *Bernhard Fromm,* born on July 20, 1898, in Berlin, died on September 22, 1954, in London; married to *Lucie Fromm,* née Freund, born on June 24, 1895, in Leipzig, died on February 14, 1988, in London. Their marriage produced:

8.1 *Frank Fromm,* born on July 27, 1930, in Berlin, died on February 14, 1988, in London. Married to *Marika Fromm,* née Kiaschek, born on July 25, 1940, in Budapest, lives in London. Their marriage produced *Anita Fromm,* who lives in Potters Bar (Great Britain).

AdK-W Akademie der Künste, West Berlin (Academy of Arts, West Berlin)

BA Bundesarchiv Berlin, Bezirksamt (Berlin Federal Archives; District Office)

BGB Bürgerliches Gesetzbuch (German Civil Code)

BLHA Brandenburgisches Landeshauptarchiv Potsdam (Central Archives of the State of Brandenburg, Potsdam)

GStA Geheimes Staatsarchiv, Berlin (State Archives for Classified Documents, Berlin)

HRB Handelsregister Berlin (Company Register)

LEA Landesentschädigungsamt Berlin (Regional Restitution Office, Berlin)

LAB Landesarchiv Berlin (State Archives, Berlin)

OFP Der Oberfinanzpräsident (Chief Finance Authority)

PrAdK Preussische Akademie der Künste, Berlin (Prussian Academy of Arts, Berlin)

RA Rechtsanwalt (Attorney)

RFM Reichsfinanzministerium (Reich Finance Ministry)

RGBl. Reichsgesetzblatt (Reich Law Gazette)
RKG Reichs-Kredit-Gesellschaft, Berlin
RM Reichsmarks
RWM Reichswirtschaftsministerium (Reich Economics Ministry)
SAdK Stiftung Archiv der Akademie der Künste, Berlin (Archives of the Foundation of the Academy of Arts, Berlin)

1. *Der Drogenhändler,* no. 23, March 20, 1933, p. 616.
2. Schivelbusch, p. 267; Laqueur, p. 225; Birett, passim; for information on the sexology bookshop, see *Der Schundkampf,* no. 50, Feb. 1933, pp. 10, 19.
3. Bertram to the Reich Minister of the Interior on May 27, 1921, BA R 1501/111891, pp. 322–324; Hirschfeld, *Geschlechtskunde,* vol. 2, p. 447; Wolf, p. 119; *Jüdisches Lexikon,* vol. 4,2 entry on "Statistik der Juden (Europa: Deutschland)," p. 641 (Berlin 1927, rpt. Frankfurt 1987).
4. Schäfer, pp. 94–96; Friedländer, p. 47; Reich Anti-Smut Bureau to the Prussian Ministry of the Interior, dated April 1, 1933, GStA I HA Rep. 77, 2772/11, vol. 1; *Der Schundkampf,* no. 9, Dec. 1925, p. 10; no. 41, July/Aug. 1931; no. 52, July 1933, pp. 8ff.; no. 54, Dec. 1933, p. 8.
5. Otto Adler commenting on the expert opinions rendered by Medical Privy Councilor Prof. Dr. E. Bumm, Health Adviser Dr. Franz Lehmann, Prof. Dr. Mackenrodt, Health Adviser Dr. Schäffer, and Prof. Dr. Strassmann, in *Zeitschrift für Sexualwissenschaft* 1

(1914), p. 186f.; draft of a law regarding business pertaining to birth control methods [June 1917], GStA Rep. 76 VIII B/2017, pp. 189–195.

6. Hirschfeld/Gaspar, vol. 1, p. 238; *Dokumentation zur Geschichte des Kondoms*, p. 4; Marcuse, passim; Woycke, p. 51; Prussian Ministry of the Interior, Minutes of the Session on May 26, 1916, to combat the decline in birth rates, GStA Rep. 76 VIII B/2017, pp. 20–26.

7. For example, in *Die Aufklärung*, 1 (1929), no. 1, p. 98.

8. Advertisement in *Das Drogisten-Fachblatt*, 1932, no. 11, p. 8 (emphasis in original), no. 5, p. 6.

9. The expropriation file of the OFP Berlin-Brandenburg, BLHA Rep. 36 A II/10607, pp. 11ff. contains an incomplete list of Fromm's patents. (Numerous Fromm patents, including the one cited here, can be found at http://depatisnet.dpma.de.)

10. Richmond, p. 501.

11. Registry of births in the Konin synagogue community, Archivum Panstwowe, Poznan, 45/66/4 (marriage entry), 48/10/19 (birth entry). For the translation of these texts, we would like to thank Jakov Kolodizner of Berlin, who served as a Red Army soldier and fought for his country at the Battle of Stalingrad, where he was severely wounded. He ultimately helped liberate the Germans from themselves.

12. Sommerfeld, p. 5f.; see also Schade.

13. Eschelbacher, *Die ostjüdische Einwanderungsbevölkerung*, pp. 40ff. Klara Eschelbacher was born in 1889, the daughter of Rabbi Dr. Joseph Eschelbacher and his wife, Ernestine, née Benario, in Bruchsal, Germany. Her dissertation adviser was Heinrich Herkner in Berlin, who noted in his evaluation: "The author has such strong personal contacts with this social group that she was able to shed a remarkable degree of light on the subject. Out of consideration for the parties involved, of course, she is unable to report everything she observed." Herkner's evaluation, dated July 27, 1918 (second reader Max Sering: "Agreed, Octo-

ber 17, 1918"), Humboldt University in Berlin, Archiv Phil. Fak. 597, Littr. P. no. 4/388, p. 337f.

14. Eschelbacher, "Wohnungsfrage," p. 256; Eschelbacher, *Die ostjüdische Einwanderungsbevölkerung,* p. 42.

15. Quoted in Fraenkel, p. 136.

16. Advertisements for Fromms Act, in *Der Drogenhändler,* Oct. 9 and Dec. 4, 1919, p. 941, 1181.

17. Advertisement by the I. Fromm company, *Der Drogenhändler,* September 27, 1917, p. viii.

18. Quotations regarding the production and testing processes are found in *Fromms Act;* "Vom Werdegang des Präservativs"; Hirschfeld, *Geschlechtskunde,* vol. 2, pp. 447–449; the information about the poster campaign for "our business associates" in *Das Drogisten-Fachblatt,* 1931, no. 8, p. 4. Emphasis in original.

19. Chief administrative officer of Potsdam, BLHA Rep. 2A I St, naturalization, Fromm Israel Julius, pp. 1–46.

20. Land register files for Rolandstr. 4, pp. 80, 88, district court of Berlin-Schöneberg, Lichterfelde branch office.

21. Industry Supervisory Board of Treptow-Köpenick; commercial regulations dated March 14, 1922, Köpenick district office, Berlin building and housing authority, construction records for Verlängerte Rahnsdorfer Str. 53/Werlseestr. 62, vols. 1, 2, 5.

22. *Niederbarnimer Zeitung,* April 11, 1927, and October 23, 1928.

23. German Credit Bureau, in the matter of Fromms Act and Julius Fromm, factory owner, February 8, 1933, BA R 8136/2994.

24. Dietrich, pp. 1-8.

25. Mies van der Rohe, p. 70; Korn, *Glass in Modern Architecture,* pp. 5ff.

26. "Werdegang des Präservativs"; Fromms Act.

27. Korn/Housden, pp. 113–135; *International Congress for Modern Architecture,* p. 106; Poelzig in a statement for the Prussian Academy of Arts on October 3, 1932, SAdK, PrAdK, 940/6.

28. Weitzmann, p. 64; Warhaftig, p. 278f.

29. Benton, p. 177; correspondence between Taut and Korn in Spring 1963; SAdK, staff news, AdK-W, 265; Weitzmann to Korn, January

23, 1937, The Jewish National and University Library, Jerusalem, Weitzmann estate, 2665/30.

30. Notification from the Office for the Settlement of Disputed Property Claims, Berlin-Mitte-Prenzlauer Berg (AROV I), dated July 13, 1994, GZ AROV I D 5-Reg. 2597/3; reference files of Benoit-Raukopf, Esq. (Berlin).

31. Advertisements for Fromms Act and for Fromms, Inc. in *Der Drogenhändler*, January 5 and 30, May 25, July 13, 1933, front pages.

32. Foreign exchange inspection of Fromms Act on February 22 and 23, and March 9, 1934, with reference to earlier inspections (signed: Müller); report from the foreign exchange inspection of Erfurt Rubber Works, Inc., dated April 19, 1934 (signed: St. Insp. Behnke), BLHA Rep. 36 A II/1557, pp. 170, 188ff.

33. BLHA, Rep. 2 A I St, Naturalization of Fromm, Israel Julius, pp. 47–102.

34. Advertisements for Fromms, Inc., in *Drogisten Zeitung, Zentralorgan der deutschen Drogistenschaft*, 60 (1934), nos. 5–8, 11, 17, 28, 30, 32, 45, 51, 52; *Deutsche Drogistenschaft*, no. 21, 1935; Fromm's 1936 Nahverkehrsplan: LAB, F Rep. 270 A 2344; RKG (Jannsen) to I. G.-Farben (von Meister), dated August 3, 1937, BA R 8136/2994. The quotations that follow are from the same file unless otherwise indicated.

35. See http://depatisnet.dpma.de.

36. *Der Stürmer*, nos. 23, 30, 34, 39 (June–Sept. 1936); we would like to thank Christoph Kreutzmüller (Berlin) for bringing this information to our attention.

37. Jaffa had served as legal counsel for the Osram lighting company until 1933. Osram, like Leiser, Ohrenstein & Koppel—and, of course, Fromms Act—was classified as a Jewish company. Bowing to political pressure, these companies began letting Jewish employees go in 1933 (see Barkai, p. 42). In 1934, Fromm employed only five Jews: a lawyer and four sales representatives.

38. RKG note dated June 10, 1938, BA R 8136/2994; on the Aryanization of Ebro, BA R 8136/3385.

39. German Credit Bureau, regarding Fromms Act and Julius Fromm, dated February 2, 1933; RA Schöne to RWM (Marwede) concerning prospective expatriate buyers holding foreign currency, dated July 18, 1938, BA R 8136/2994.

40. RA Coper (Berlin) to BA Köpenick, dated July 11, 1946; statement by Genth, dated July 9, 1948, LAB C Rep. 105/1822; RWM (Marwede) to v. Epenstein-Mauternburg, care of Metz-Randa, dated September 30, 1939, BLHA Rep. 361/1557, p. 44f.; OFP Berlin to Epenstein-Mauternburg, dated June 9, 1939, BLHA Rep. 36 A II/10607, p. 90.

41. Sales negotiations by the RKG 1937/38 BA R 8136/2994. Julius Fromm's lawyer, Sally Jaffa, who was also present, later described the process in similar terms (RA Hans Noltenius to restitution office in Berlin-Schöneberg, dated February 9, 1951, LAB B Rep. 025-06, 6 WAG 765/50, p. 39f.); certified signature from the Berlin commercial register, October 1, 1948; RA Coper to BA Berlin-Köpenick, July 11, 1946; special audit of Fromms Act Rubber Factory VEB by the Greater Berlin city council, bureau for regulation of state-owned companies (Foige), January 15, 1951, LAB C Rep. 105/1822; Berlin commercial register (92 HBR 7762), excerpts, LEA Berlin Reg. no. 53154.

42. Reich Economics Ministry (Marwede) to von Epenstein-Mauternburg and Metz-Randa, regarding *Entjudung* (exclusion of the Jews) from Fromms Act Rubber Factory, Inc., dated September 30, 1938, BLHA Rep. 36 A II/1557, p. 44f.

43. RA Coper to Köpenick district office, dated July 11, 1945, LAB Rep. 105/1822.

44. Special audit of Fromms Act Rubber Works VEB by the Berlin city council, finance department, HA publicly owned assets (Foige), dated January 15, 1951; LAB C Rep. 105/1822, p. 51.

45. Köpenick district office of the Berlin building and housing authority; construction files for Friedrichshagener Strasse, 2653, vol. 13.

46. Seidler, p. 293.

47. Chief Executive Officer Viert to the building inspection department in Berlin-Köpenick, dated October 4, 1930, Köpenick district office of Berlin, building and housing authority, Friedrichshagener Strasse 38, vol. IV; Viert to the building inspection department in Berlin-Köpenick, dated October 12, 1938, ibid., vol. XII.

48. Quoted in Overy, p. 19.

49. Herzog, pp. 219-237.

50. On Göring's and Epenstein's family history, see Overy, p. 11; Maser, p. 15; Gritzbach, p. 222f.; Irving, p. 41; Lange, p. 180. See also Emmy Göring, *An der Seite meines Mannes*; interviews with L. Schroth and S. Krassauer; on the Aryanization of the estate in Gösing, see Gamsjäger, p. 136f.

51. This quotation and the two that follow are in London, pp. 106, 30, 43.

52. Report by Alexander Fromm, n.d., LAB B Rep. 025-06, 6 WAG 1667-95/51, p. 16f.

53. Copy of the bill of sale, dated January 17, 1939, LAB B Rep. 025-6, 6 WGA 1944/51, vol. 1, p. 88f.; sworn statement by Leo Lippmann, soap maker, dated January 13, 1956; ibid., p. 88m; statement by the Berlin chief of police, dated January 24, 1939, copy; ibid., p. 101; Berlin chief of police to Fromms Act, Inc., dated December 21, 1940, LAB B Rep. 025-06, WAG 8778/59.

54. Julius Fromm to his daughter-in-law Paulette Fromm in Paris, dated June 8, 1940, original in English. Estate of Paulette Fromm, in the possession of Henri Fromm (Paris).

55. Lafitte, p. 62.

56. Soukup, pp. 83ff.

57. Edgar Fromm's experiences and observations during his internment in England and Australia at the beginning of the war 1939/40, recorded by W. Berent, Wiener Library, London, P III.i. (England), no. 604.

58. The quotations about the *Dunera* affair are found in Wilczynski, pp. 32ff. (see also Klaus Wilczynski, *Auf einmal sollst du ein Fremder sein. Eine Berliner Familiengeschichte*, Berlin: Das Neue Berlin, 1998); Bartrop/Eisen, p. 53; London, p. 171; Kolbet, passim.

59. Unless otherwise indicated, this chapter and the following one are based on expropriation files, totaling 236 pages in the first instance and 152 in the second, of the Chief Finance Authority of Berlin (later Berlin-Brandenburg) regarding the asset valuation of "expatriate Fromm, Julius Israel." They also contain records from the period of the enemy asset administration. BLHA Rep. 36 A II/10607 and 10608. Of particular interest is a currency exchange document marked "Fromm, Julius Israel, London." Ibid. Rep. 36 A G/893.

60. Merten to the director of the Berlin-Zehlendorf tax office, dated June 15, 1943, endorsed and forwarded to the OFP Berlin-Brandenburg on June 16, 1943, BLHA Rep. 36 A II/23862, p. 50.

61. Lindner, p. 141.

62. Ibid., p. 142.

63. Aly, *Hitler's Beneficiaries*, p. 195.

64. On the significance of the Municipal Pawnshop of Berlin in appraising confiscated jewelry, especially from Jews, see Aly, *Hitler's Beneficiaries*, pp. 197ff; see also Meinl/Zwilling, pp. 492–496.

65. Evidence and adjudication of the District Court of Berlin in the matter of restitution Max Fromm et al., dated January 11, 1966 (Judges: Schlecht, Schmilinsky, Schmeisser), LAB B Rep. 025-06, 61 WAG 8778/59, pp. 21f., 37, 112–121 (also 61 WAG 8780/59).

66. German Credit Bureau, regarding Fromms Act and Julius Fromm, factory owner, February 8, 1933, BA R 8136/2994.

67. OFP Berlin-Brandenburg (Thulcke) to RFM, dated February 13, 1943; RFM (Maedel) to OFP Berlin-Brandenburg, dated April 1, 1943, LAB A Rep. 093-03/54570, pp. 76–78.

68. Friedenberger et al., p. 88f.; Aly, *Hitler's Beneficiaries*, p. 68; for the wording of the stricter regulation of February 16, 1943, BA R 1501/1838, p. 21.

69. Land registry entry for Rolandstrasse 4, Division One, district court of Berlin-Schöneberg, Lichterfelde branch office.

70. Finance senator to the restitution division of the Berlin regional court, dated February 12, 1954, LAB Rep. 025-08, 8 WGA 7/50, p. 120. For a general and instructive overview of the personal

profit of Nazi officials and on the "endowments" for loyal Nazi officers, see Bajohr.

71. Klemperer, vol. 2, pp. 171, 137.

72. For an overview of this issue, see Aly, *Hitler's Beneficiaries*, pp. 117–131; for a detailed analysis of one individual case, see Aly, *Into the Tunnel*, pp. 37–82.

73. Sworn statement by Max Fromm, 1963. Compensation claim filed by Herbert Fromm on December 31, 1957, LAB B Rep. 025-0661, WAG 8778/59.

74. Aly, *Hitler's Beneficiaries*, p. 124. (The official number of freight cars—528—was actually 10 percent higher; these additional freight cars were brought to central storage areas for cities at particularly high risk.)

75. Final notification concerning the compensation claims filed by the Fromm community of heirs on October 9, 1962, finance senator (Berlin) to the regional compensation bureau in Berlin on February 24, 1955; Loebinger to Fromm on February 24, 1939, LEA Reg. no. 53154; OFP Berlin-Brandenburg, Asset Valuation Office, Fromm, Ruth, BLHA Rep. 36 A II/10612.

76. Compensation proceedings for Ruth Fromm, BLA B Rep. 025-06, 62 WAG 799/57, p. 6.

77. RA Hans Noltenius to the 44th Restitution Division of the District Court of Berlin, dated April 6, 1951, LAB B Rep. 025-06, 6 WGA 765/50, p. 79.

78. Death certificate for Berthold Fromm, BLHA Rep. 35 H KZ Sachsenhausen/319.

79. Naujoks, pp. 303ff.; Scheffler, pp. 105ff.

80. OFP files for Jenny Steinfeld et al., BLHA Rep. 36 A II/36982 and 24897.

81. Expropriation file of Jenny Steinfeld, BLHA Rep. 36 A II/36982, p. 22.

82. Sworn testimony of Leo Lippmann, January 13, 1956, LAB B Rep. 025-06, 6 WGA 1944/51, vol. 1, p. 88m; expropriation file of Willy and Esther [Else] Brandenburg, BLHA Rep. 36 A II/4673.

83. Sworn statement by Elsbeth Fromm (née Kuntze), on January 12, 1960, BLA B Rep. 025-06, 62 WAG 799/57, p. 28f.; communication from Ruth Fromm, who spoke to this concierge in 1945.

84. Czech, p. 434.

85. Gestapo Berlin to OFP Berlin-Brandenburg on April 21, 1943, BLHA Rep. 36 A II/24897, p. 21a.

86. Max Fromm to Wolfheim, dated June 26, 1950. Henri Fromm (Paris) has kept a copy of this letter, on which the preceding account is based.

87. Résumé of Siegfried Fromm, dated November 5, 1945, LAB C Rep. 118-01, no. 38685; Sunniva Graefe, sworn statement dated January 9, 1956, OAB B Rep. 025-26, 6 WGA 1944/51, vol. 1, p. 88k; letter from Alfred Fromm to his mother, written in Balz on May 11, 1943, property of Ilse Fromm (Munich).

88. Nagel, *Geschichte MAPA's*, published in serial form in *Gummilinse*, August, October, and December 1991.

89. License agreement, Metz-Randa's appeal, the subsequent written statements by attorneys Walter Fuhrmann (Berlin) and Hans Noltenius (Bremen), and the final settlement on June 27, 1951, LAB B Rep. 025-06, 6 WGA 765/50.

90. Advertising brochure for the Hanseatic Rubber Company (1948).

91. Details about the nature of these attacks can be found at www.angelfire.com/super/ussbs/ussbsappc.html; for information about the repercussions for Fromms Act, see LAB A Rep. 005-07/274.

92. Unless otherwise indicated, the following details are based on files at the Berlin municipal authority, finance dept., LAB C Rep. 105/1822/43204/43205.

93. Order no. 124, issued by the commander-in-chief of the Soviet occupying troops in Germany on October 30, 1945.

94. Report by Fritz Schmitt, chief engineer, Berlin, written on January 24, 1934 at the request of the Prussian chief administrative officer in Potsdam, BLHA, Rep. 2A I St, naturalization of Fromm, Israel Julius, p. 68.

95. Will drawn up by Julius Fromm on December 12, 1944, in London, estate of Edgar Fromm, in the possession of Raymond Fromm (London); Julius Fromm to Max and Paulette Fromm on February 6, 1945, estate of Max Fromm, in the possession of Henri Fromm (Paris).

Akademie der Künste (1970–1979). Vol. 4: *Nachrufe*. Berlin: Akademie der Künste, 1980.

Aly, Götz. *Into the Tunnel: The Brief Life of Marion Samuel, 1931–1943*. Trans. Ann Millin. New York: Metropolitan Books, 2008.

———. *Hitler's Beneficiaries: Plunder, Racial War, and the Nazi Welfare State*. Trans. Jefferson Chase. New York: Metropolitan Books, 2007.

Bajohr, Frank. *Parvenüs und Profiteure: Korruption in der NS-Zeit*. Frankfurt: S. Fischer, 2001.

Barkai, Avraham. *From Boycott to Annihilation: The Economic Struggle of German Jews, 1933–1948*. Trans. William Templer. Hanover, NH: Univ. Press of New England, 1989.

Bartrop, Paul R., and Gabrielle Eisen, eds. *The Dunera Affair: A Documentary Resource Book*. Melbourne: Schwartz & Wilkinson: Jewish Museum of Australia, 1990.

Bauer, Marianne Ursula, and Lutz Kohlschmidt. *Die Frommser-Saga: Alles über Kondome von A bis Z*. Leipzig: Neuer Sachsenverlag, 1991.

Benton, Charlotte. *A Different World: Émigré Architects in Britain 1928–1958*. London: RIBA Heinz Gallery, 1995.

Bertschi, Hannes. *Die Kondom-Story.* Cologne: VGS Verlagsanstalt, 1994.

Birett, Herbert, ed. *Verbotene Druckschriften in Deutschland: Eine Dokumentation.* Vol. 2: Schmutz und Schund [rpt. of the catalogue by the German Central Police Bureau to Stem the Circulation of Lewd Pictures, Literature, and Advertisements compiled at the Prussian police headquarters in Berlin, 1926, with supplements in 1926 and 1936]. Vaduz: Topos Ruggell, 1995.

Czech, Danuta. *Auschwitz Chronicle 1939–1945.* New York: Owl Books, 1997.

Dietrich, Ulf. "Architekten Arthur Korn und Dipl.-Ing. Weitzmann, Berlin. Gummifabrik in Köpenick." In *Bauwelt* 1931, no. 15, pp. 1–8.

Dokumentation zur Geschichte des Kondoms. Erstellt aus Anlass des 75-jährigen Jubiläums der Marke Fromms 1914 bis 1994. Zeven: n.p., 1995.

Eschelbacher, Klara. *Die ostjüdische Einwanderungsbevölkerung der Stadt Berlin.* Diss. Berlin, 1920.

———. "Die Wohnungsfrage." In *Neue Jüdische Monatshefte,* 1920, no. 11, pp. 255–261.

Fraenkel, Ludwig. *Die Empfängnisverhütung: Biologische Grundlagen, Technik und Indikationen; Für Ärzte bearbeitet.* Stuttgart: Ferdinand Enke Verlag, 1932.

Friedenberger, Martin, Klaus-Dieter Gössel, Eberhard Schönknecht, eds. *Die Reichsfinanzverwaltung im Nationalsozialismus: Darstellung und Dokumente.* Bremen: Edition Temmen, 2002.

Friedländer, Saul. *Kurt Gerstein: The Ambiguity of Good.* New York: Alfred A. Knopf, 1969.

Fromms Act. Gummiwerke Berlin-Cöpenick—Berlin-Friedrichshagen in *Archiv für Industrie und Handel,* vol. 2. Berlin, 1930 [found as an offprint at the Leipzig German Library; call number: 1931 C 25].

Gamsjäger, Bernhard. "Vom Kruckenkreuz zum Hakenkreuz," in Gamsjäger, *Puchenstuben.* Puchenstuben: Gemeinde Puchstuben, 2004, pp. 129–136.

Geisel, Eike. *Im Scheunenviertel—Bilder, Texte und Dokumente.* Berlin: Siedler, 1981.

Göring, Emmy. *An der Seite meines Mannes: Begebenheiten und Bekennt-nisse.* Göttingen: Schültz, 1967.

Gritzbach, Erich. *Hermann Goering: The Man and His Work; The Only Authorized Biography.* Trans. Gerald Griffin. New York: AMS Press, 1973.

Grossmann, Atina. *Reforming Sex: The German Movement for Birth Control and Abortion Reform 1920–1950.* New York: Oxford Univ. Press, 1997.

Herzog, Lorenz Peter. *Im Schatten des Ötschers: Roman aus dem Alpen-lande.* Vienna: St. Pöltner Verlagsanstalt, 1943.

Hirschfeld, Magnus. *Geschlechtskunde.* Vol. 2: *Folgen und Forderungen.* Stuttgart: Julius Püttmann, 1928.

Hirschfeld, Magnus, and Andreas Gaspar, eds. *Sittengeschichte des 20. Jahrhunderts.* Vol. 1: *Sittengeschichte des Ersten Weltkriegs.* Vol. 2: *Zwischen zwei Katastrophen. Sittengeschichte der Nachkriegszeit 1918–1930.* Hanau: Schustek, 1966.

Hirschfeld, Magnus, and Richard Linsert. *Empfängnisverhütung: Mittel und Methoden.* Berlin: Neuer Deutscher Verlag, 1932.

Irving, David. *Göring.* New York: Morrow, 1989.

Kirschey-Feix, Ingrid, ed. *Treffpunkt Scheunenviertel: Leben im Schtetl.* Berlin: Verlag Neues Leben, 1993.

Klemmer, Clemens. "Meister der Moderne. Arthur Korn (1891–1978). Tischler, Architekt, Städteplaner," in *Werk, Bauen, Wohnen,* 1992, vol. 10, pp. 78ff.

Klemperer, Victor. *I Will Bear Witness: The Diaries of Victor Klemperer.* Trans. Martin Chalmers. Vol. 2: Diaries 1942–1945. New York: Morrow, 1999.

Knopf, Volker, and Stefan Martens. *Görings Reich: Selbstinszenierungen in Carinhall.* Berlin: Links, 1999.

Kolbet, Christiane. "Wie es den Fürther Emil Höchster in die australische Wüste verschlug." In *Raumzeit* no. 19, December 20, 2002, http://www.raumzeit-online.de/122002.

Korn, Arthur. "Analytische und utopische Architektur," in *Kunstblatt* 1923 pp. 336–339; rpt. as "Analytical and Utopian Architecture," in

Ulrich Conrads, ed. *Programs and Manifestoes on 20th-Century Architecture.* Trans. Michael Bullock. Cambridge, MA: MIT Press, 1970, p. 71f.

———. *Glass in Modern Architecture.* London: Barrie & Rockliff, 1967.

———. "The Work of James Stirling and James Gowan," in *The Architect and Building News,* January 7, 1959, pp. 7–23.

Korn, Arthur, and Brian Housden. "Arthur Korn, 1891 to Present Day," in *Architecture Association Journal,* December 1957, pp. 113–135.

Lafitte, François. *The Internment of Aliens.* London: Libris, 1988.

Lange, Eitel. *Der Reichsmarschall im Kriege: Ein Bericht in Wort und Bild.* Stuttgart: C. E. Schwab, 1950.

Laqueur, Walter. *Weimar: A Cultural History, 1918–1933.* New York: Putnam, 1974.

Lindner, Stephan. *Das Reichskommissariat für die Behandlung feindlichen Vermögens im Zweiten Weltkrieg. Eine Studie zur Verwaltungs-, Rechts- und Wirtschaftsgeschichte des nationalsozialistischen Deutschlands.* Stuttgart: Franz Steiner Verlag, 1991.

London, Louise. *Whitehall and the Jews 1933–1948: British Immigration Policy, Jewish Refugees, and the Holocaust.* Cambridge: Cambridge Univ. Press, 2000.

MAPA, Inc., ed. *75 Jahre Fromms: Ein Kondom macht Geschichte.* Zeven, n.p., 1994.

Marcuse, Max, ed. *Handwörterbuch der Sexualwissenschaft: Enzyklopädie der natur- und kulturwissenschaftlichen Sexualkunde des Menschen.* Bonn: A. Marcus & E. Weber, 1923.

Maser, Werner. *Hermann Göring: Hitlers janusköpfiger Paladin; Die politische Biographie.* Berlin: Edition q, 2000.

Meinen, Insa. *Wehrmacht und Prostitution während des Zweiten Weltkriegs im besetzten Frankreich.* Bremen: Edition Temmen, 2002.

Meinl, Susanne, and Jutta Zwilling. *Legalisierter Raub: Die Ausplünderung der Juden durch die Reichsfinanzverwaltung in Hessen.* Frankfurt: Campus, 2004.

Mies van der Rohe, Ludwig. "Arbeitsthesen," in *G,* no. 1, 1922; rpt. in Ulrich Conrads, ed., *Programs and Manifestoes on 20th-Century Architecture.* Trans. Michael Bullock. Cambridge, MA: MIT Press, 1970.

Moderne Ladenbauten. Innen- und Aussenarchitektur, mit 180 Abb. Berlin-Charlottenburg: E. Pollack, 1928.

Nagel, Jochen. "Geschichte MAPA's," in *Gummilinse*, no. 1–3, 1991, and 1–5, 1992.

Naujoks, Harry. *Mein Leben im KZ Sachsenhausen 1936–1942: Erinnerungen des ehemaligen Lagerältesten.* Cologne: Röderberg, 1987.

Overy, Richard J. *Goering: The "Iron Man."* London and Boston: Routledge & Kegan Paul, 1984.

Parisot, Jeannette. *Johnny Come Lately: A Short History of the Condom.* Trans. Bill McCann. London: Journeyman, 1987.

Paul, Wolfgang. *Wer war Hermann Göring? Biographie.* Esslingen: Bechtle, 1983.

————. *Hermann Göring: Hitler's Paladin or Puppet.* Trans. Helmut Bögler. London: Arms & Armour Press, 1998.

Richmond, Theo. *Konin: A Quest.* New York: Pantheon, 1995.

Rosenberg, Stephen. "The Ring and Arthur Korn," in *AA Journal*, February 1958, p. 170f.

Schade, Anja. "Licht aus in der Mulackritze," in Elisabeth von Dücker, ed., *Sexarbeit. Prostitution—Lebenswelten und Mythen.* Bremen: Edition Temmen, 2005, pp. 97–99.

Schäfer, Jürgen. *Kurt Gerstein. Zeuge des Holocaust.* Bielefeld: Luther-Verlag, 1999.

Scheffler, Wolfgang. "Der Brandanschlag im Berliner Lustgarten und seine Folgen: Eine quellenkritische Betrachtung," in *Jahrbuch des Landesarchivs Berlin*, 1994, pp. 91–118.

Schivelbusch, Wolfgang. *The Culture of Defeat: On National Trauma, Mourning, and Recovery.* Trans. Jefferson Chase. New York: Metropolitan Books, 2003.

Der Schundkampf. Blatt der Reichsschundkampfstelle der ev. Jungmännerbünde Deutschlands, 1925–1933.

Seidler, Franz. *Prostitution, Homosexualität, Selbstverstümmelung: Probleme der deutschen Sanitätsführung 1939–1945.* Neckargemünd: Vowinckel, 1977.

Sharp, Dennis, ed. *Planning and Architecture: Essays Presented to Arthur Korn by the Architectural Association.* London: Barrie & Rockliff, 1967.

Sommer, Theo. *1945—Die Biographie eines Jahres*. Reinbeck: Rowohlt, 2005.

Sommerfeld, Adolf. *Das Ghetto von Berlin: Aus dem Scheunenviertel*. Berlin: Verlag Neues Leben, 1992.

Sontheimer, Michael. *Bilder des Zweiten Weltkriegs*. Munich and Hamburg: DVA, 2005.

————. "Die Fromms-Saga," in *Spiegel Spezial*, May 1, 1995.

Soukup, Uwe. *Ich bin nun mal ein Deutscher: Sebastian Haffner; Eine Biographie*. Berlin: Aufbau, 2001.

Steinmann, Martin, ed. *C.I.A.M. Dokumente 1928–1939*. Basel: Birkhäuser, 1997.

"Vom Werdegang des Präservativs," in *Der Drogenhändler*, 1931, no. 57, p. 1627f.

Warhaftig, Myra. *Deutsche jüdische Architekten vor und nach 1933: Das Lexikon; 500 Biographien*. Berlin: Dietrich Reimer, 2005.

Weeks, Jeffrey. *Sex, Politics, and Society: The Regulation of Sexuality since 1800*. New York: Longman, 1981.

Weitzmann, Siegfried. *Studie über Kafka*. Foreword by Robert Weltsch. Tel Aviv: Edition Olamenu, 1970.

Wilczynski, Klaus. *Das Gefangenenschiff: Mit der "Dunera" über vier Weltmeere*. Berlin: Verlag am Park, 2001.

Wolf, Julius. *Der Geburtenrückgang. Die Rationalisierung des Geschlechtslebens in unserer Zeit*. Jena: Fischer, 1912.

Woycke, James. *Birth Control in Germany, 1871–1933*. London and New York: Routledge, 1988.

Zadek, Alice and Gerhard. *Mit dem letzten Zug nach England: Opposition, Exil, Heimkehr*. Berlin: Dietz, 1992.

Zborowski, Mark and Elisabeth Herzog. *Life Is With People: The Culture of the Shtetl*. New York: Schocken, 1995.

Interview with Edgar Fromm by Michael Sontheimer on February 21,
1995, in London

Interview with Ruth Fromm by Hannah Kruse on April 17, 2005, in
New York

Interview with Raymond Fromm by Michael Sontheimer on February
2, 2006, in London

Interview with Thomas Harder, head of the condom division of MAPA,
Inc., by Michael Sontheimer on March 16, 2006, in Zeven

Telephone interview with Sieglinde Krassauer, manager of the Gösing
Alpenhotel for many years, by Michael Sontheimer on March 27,
2006

Interview with Ruth Fromm by Götz Aly on April 12, 2006, in New York

Interview with Henri Fromm by Michael Sontheimer on April 14, 2006,
in Charroux

Interview with Liselotte Schroth, niece of Elisabeth Epenstein, by Michael
Sontheimer on May 4, 2006, in Mauterndorf

Interview with Ilse Fromm by Michael Sontheimer on May 7, 2006,
in Munich

ACKNOWLEDGMENTS

A GUEST PROFESSORSHIP for interdisciplinary Holocaust research at the Fritz Bauer Institute of the University of Frankfurt provided Götz Aly indispensable financial and academic support for this book. The Spiegel Verlag allowed Michael Sontheimer to take a three-month sabbatical. The authors would also like to thank the following individuals for their kind assistance: Lisa Abramson, Petra Benoit-Raukopf, Henri Fromm, Ilse Fromm, Raymond Fromm, and Ruth Fromm; Jakov Kolodizner, Hannah Kruse, Astrid Proll and her students at the Ostkreuz School of Photography, Claus Richter, Sabine Sauer, Ilse Schroth, Elke Schmitter, Katharina Steinberg, Maritta Tkalec, and Klaus Wilczynski; Marion Kühnhausen (archivist at the construction and housing department of the Berlin-Köpenick district office), Katrin Grün, Anke Kandler, and Monika Nakath (Central Archives of the State of Brandenburg, Potsdam), Barbara Welker (Centrum Judaicum, Berlin), Feliks Tych (Jewish Historical Institute, Warsaw), Aubrey Pomerance (Jewish Museum, Berlin), Klaus Dettmer, Heike Schroll, and Bianca Welzing (State Archives, Berlin), and Helga Gappmayer (Lungau Regional Museum, Mauterndorf).

p. ix: Raymond Fromm; **p. 3:** Raymond Fromm; **p. 5:** from *Das Drogisten-Fachblatt* 4/1930; **p. 10:** from Hirschfeld/Gaspar, *Sittengeschichte*, p. 242 [originally from A.I.Z.]; **p. 11:** from Hirschfeld/Gaspar, p. 353; **p. 14:** from Friedrichspalast Berlin, p. 18; **p. 19:** from Richmond, picture #20; **p. 24:** Jüdisches Museum Berlin (JMB); **p. 25:** JMB; **p. 26:** Henri Fromm; **p. 30:** Raymond Fromm; **p. 32:** from *Der Drogenhändler*, Sept. 27, 1917; **p. 33:** Henri Fromm; **p. 36:** Henri Fromm; **p. 38:** Henri Fromm; **p. 40:** Henri Fromm; **pp. 40–48:** JMB; **pp. 49 and 50:** Henri Fromm; **p. 55:** Landesarchiv Berlin; **pp. 57 and 58:** Henri Fromm; **p. 59:** from Korn, *Glass*, p. 43; **p. 60 (left):** from Weitzmann; **p. 60 (right):** from Warhaftig, p. 275; **p. 62:** from *Bauwelt*, 16/1931; **p. 66:** Henri Fromm; **p. 69:** from *Der deutsche Drogist*, 1/1937, p. 3; **p. 70:** from *Der deutsche Drogist*, 1/1937, p. 3; **p. 73 and 74:** Henri Fromm; **p. 77:** Henri Fromm; **p. 81:** Helga Gappmayer; **p. 82:** Michael Sontheimer; **pp. 84 and 85:** Helga Gappmayer; **p. 87 (left):** Helga Gappmayer; **p. 87 (right):** Ilse Schroth; **p. 89:** Ilse Schroth; **p. 93:** Henri Fromm; **p. 95:** JMB; **pp. 97 and 98:** from *Moderne Ladenbauten*, pp. 80 and 81; **p. 103:** www.bluestarline.org; **p. 104:** www.aufrichtigs.com; **p. 106:** Raymond

Fromm; **p. 111:** Finanzgeschichtliche Sammlung der Bundesfinan-zakademie; **p. 115:** Henri Fromm; **p. 118:** Henri Fromm; **p. 123:** Michael Sontheimer; **p. 125:** Film-Foto-Verlag, postcard, Berlin, n.d.; **p. 132:** Stadtarchiv Oberhausen; **p. 138:** JMB; **pp. 142 and 143:** JMB; **p. 147:** Henri Fromm; **p. 150:** Raymond Fromm; **pp. 152–155:** JMB; **p. 159:** MAPA, Inc.; **p. 162:** Claus Richter; **p. 170:** Henri Fromm.